Kingfisher first encyclopedia

KINGFISHER

Project Editor Tara Benson
Project Designer Siân Williams

Editorial Manager Sue Grabham

Editors Sue Barraclough, Charlotte Evans, Debbie Fox
Proofreader Jill Somerscales

Additional Design Kelly Flynn
Art Editor Sue Aldworth
Additional art preparation Ruth Levy
DTP Operator Tracey McNerney

Photography Tim Ridley, Nick Goodall
Prop organizer Sarah Wilson

Picture Research Image Select, London

Artwork Archivist Wendy Allison
Assistant Artwork Archivist Steve Robinson

Production Manager Susan Latham

Cover Design Mike Yuen

Writers Anne Civardi, Ruth Thomson

General Consultant Margaret Mallet PhD

Specialist Consultants
Michael Chinery BSc (Natural Sciences)
Keith Lye BA FRGS (Geography)
Peter Mellett BSc (Science and Technology)
James Muirden BEd (Astronomy)
Dr Elizabeth McCall Smith MB ChB MRCGP DRCOG (Human Body)
Julia Stanton BA DipEd (Australasia)
Philip Steele BA (History and the Arts)
Dr David Unwin BSc PhD (Palaeontology)

KINGFISHER

First published 1996 by Kingfisher
an imprint of Macmillan Children's Books
a division of Macmillan Publishers Limited
20 New Wharf Road, London N1 9RR
Basingstoke and Oxford
Associated companies throughout the world
www.panmacmillan.com

ISBN 978-07534-3289-1

1 3 5 7 9 10 8 6 4 2
1TF/0211/WKT/PICA/105MA

A CIP catalogue record for this book is available from the British Library
Printed in China

Your book

Your *First Encyclopedia* is packed with exciting information, amazing facts and colourful pictures. All your favourite topics appear in alphabetical order. The topics are listed on the next two pages. This page will show you how to use your book.

string puppets

◁ Information is written above, below or next to each picture. Use the arrows to find out which picture to look at.

▷ Look out for the numbered pictures. The numbers will help you to look at the pictures in the right order.

Fact box

These boxes are full of important information. They will tell you all about

- sizes
- weights
- measurements
- comparisons
- dates

◁ Follow the lines to find out where the pedal, saddle, safety helmet and handlebar are. Many of the pictures are labelled in this way.

◁ When you see these children, turn to the next page for more information on the same topic.

Find out more

If you want to find out more about each topic, look at this box. The list will show you which pages to look at.

Contents

Africa

Africa is the second largest and the warmest continent in the world. It has hot deserts, thick rainforests and flat grasslands where many animals live. Many different peoples live in Africa. Most Africans live in the countryside and are farmers, but more and more are moving to the cities to find work.

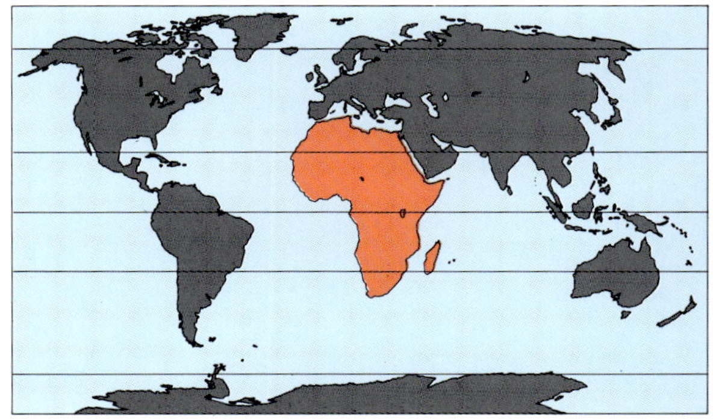

△ On this map, Africa is shown in red. Africa is joined to Asia and a thin sea separates it from Europe.

▽ This man sells water to thirsty people who pass by. Water is very valuable in the desert.

◁ The Sahara is the world's biggest desert. It covers nearly one third of Africa. It also has the highest sand dunes in the world.

△ Cairo is the capital city of Egypt. It is also the largest city in Africa. It is a dusty and crowded city with lots of traffic.

▷ In many villages, women share the work of preparing meals together. Here they are pounding maize into flour to make pancakes.

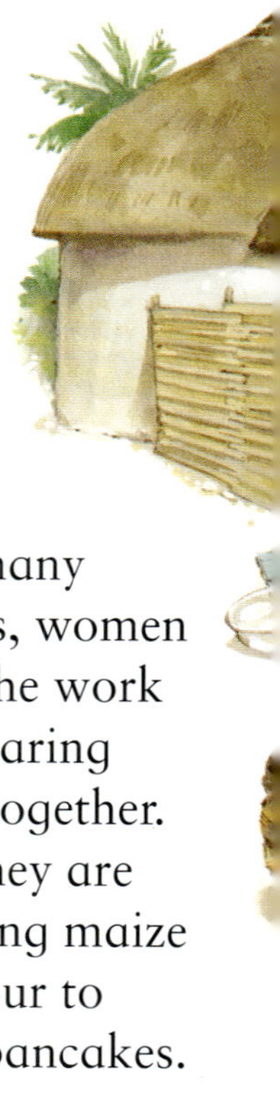

▷ Many of the world's finest diamonds come from South Africa. They are found buried deep inside rocks.

▷ This beautiful bottle is made out of a gourd, a plant like a pumpkin. It was made in Kenya and has a stopper shaped like a head.

▷ Africa's large grasslands are home to many animals, like these elephants. People also graze cattle on the grassland.

△ Maputo is the capital city of Mozambique in south-east Africa. It has many high-rise buildings and a busy port.

Find out more
Art
Grasslands
History
Water
World

Air

Air is totally invisible. You cannot see, smell or taste it, but it is all around you. Air has no shape. It pushes out in all directions and fills every space.

Air is made up of gases. One of them is called oxygen. People and animals need to breathe in oxygen to stay alive.

parachute

◁ A parachute comes down slowly because air pushes up against it.

seagull

▷ Birds can glide for miles on warm, rising air because warm air moves upwards.

kite

▷ Wind is moving air. It keeps a kite flying in the sky. If the wind stops blowing the kite will crash down to the ground.

▷ When you blow up a balloon, air is squashed inside it. If you blow it up too much, the air pushes against the balloon and bursts it.

Find out more
Earth
Energy
Flying machines
Human body
Weather

Amphibians

Frogs, toads, salamanders and newts are all amphibians. Most amphibians are born in water. As they grow they change so that they can also live on land. The largest amphibian is the Japanese giant salamander, which can grow up to one and a half metres long.

◁ A frog has smooth, slimy skin. It leaps with its long back legs.

frog

toad

▷ A toad has a fat body with rough, dry skin. It often lives in drier places than a frog.

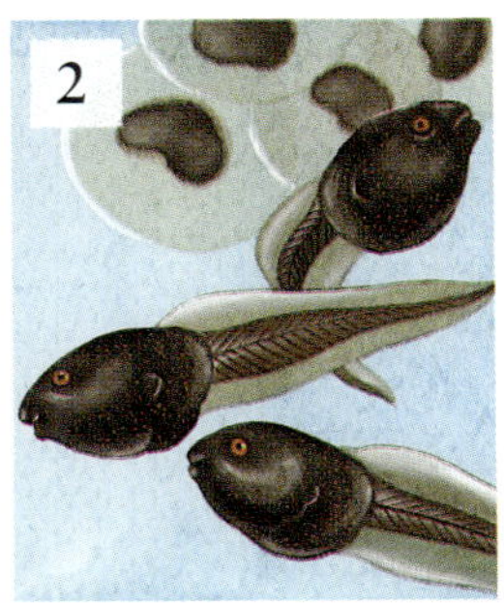

△ **1** In spring, female frogs lay their eggs in water. **2** The eggs hatch into tadpoles with wriggly tails.

△ **3** The tadpoles grow fatter and their legs appear. **4** Once they lose their tails the frogs can leave the water to look for food.

▽ Most salamanders and newts lay eggs in water. They grow in the same way as frogs and toads, but they do not lose their tails.

long-tailed salamander

great crested newt

Fact box

- An amphibian is cold-blooded. This means that the temperature of its body stays the same as the air or water around it.
- Amphibians have backbones, so they are called vertebrates.

Find out more
Animals
Prehistoric life
Water

Animals

Animals are living things that get their energy to move and grow from eating food. They are all shapes and sizes – from enormous whales to animals so tiny that thousands would fit on to a teaspoon. Some animals even live inside other animals and plants. Animals can be found all over the world – in hot, dry deserts, in icy oceans and on freezing cold mountaintops.

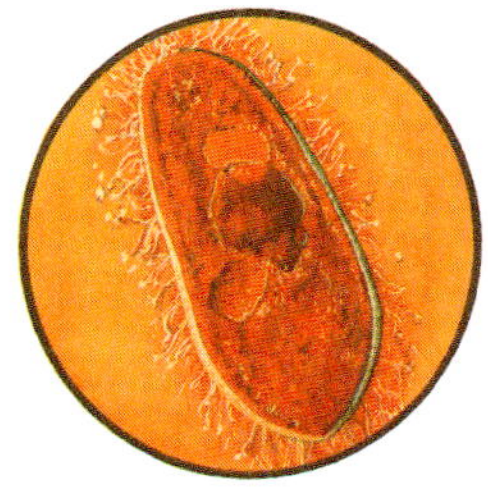

△ This animal is so small that it can be seen only through a microscope.

Fact box

- There are about one and a half million different kinds of animal in the world.
- The two main groups of animals are vertebrates and invertebrates. A vertebrate has a backbone and an invertebrate does not.
- Some animals eat meat, some eat plants and some eat meat and plants.

▽ Blue whales are the biggest animals that ever lived on Earth. Adult blue whales are larger than any of the dinosaurs ever were.

blue whales

Animals in the air
Most animals that have wings can fly. Moths and bats usually fly around at night. Falcons and most other birds fly in the daytime to find food. Falcons swoop down to catch prey.

moth

falcon

long-eared bat

Animals on land
Stocky wombats shuffle slowly. They go into underground burrows if they are scared. Zebras are able to gallop away from danger. Snakes can slither quickly across the ground.

zebra

coral snake

wombats

Animals in water
Jellyfish pump water through their bodies to push themselves along. Crabs scuttle sideways across the sea bed. Fish swim along by moving their tails from side to side.

jellyfish

angel fish

crab

Vertebrates

Animals that have a backbone are called vertebrates.

gila monster

△ **Reptiles** are cold-blooded. They need heat from the Sun to keep warm.

tree frog

△ **Amphibians** can live in the water and on land. They usually lay their eggs in water, but spend most of their time on land.

monkey

△ **Mammals** usually have hair or fur to keep them warm. Babies are cared for by their mothers and feed on their mothers' milk.

stickleback

△ **Fish** live in water. They breathe with gills, which are slits just behind their heads. Their bodies are covered in tiny scales.

hummingbird

◁ **Birds** are covered with feathers and have wings. Most birds can fly. All birds have beaks, or bills, instead of teeth.

Invertebrates
Animals without backbones are called invertebrates.

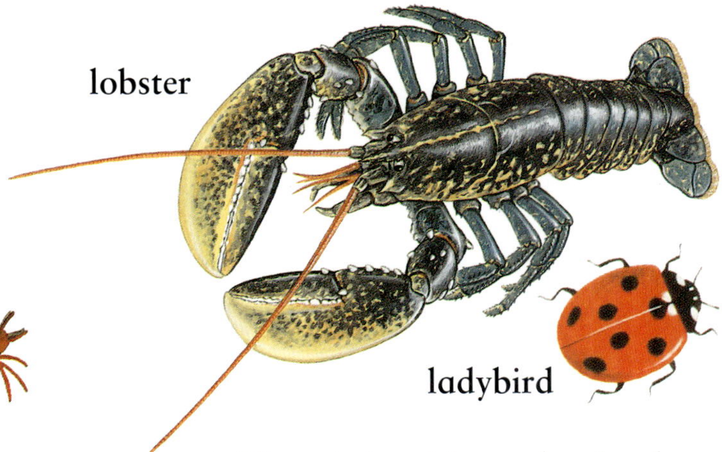

lobster

ladybird

△ These **jointed-legged animals** have tough outer skins to protect their soft bodies. Their legs are jointed, like a suit of armour, so that they can move.

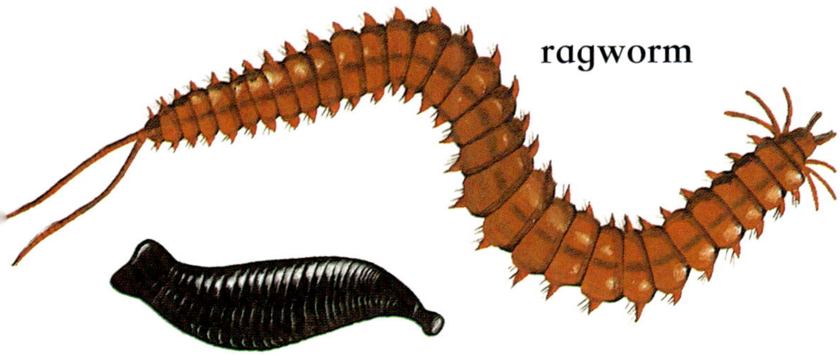

ragworm

leech

△ **Worms** have long, thin, soft bodies with no legs. Their bodies are made up of segments.

sea urchin

starfish

△ **Spiny-skinned animals** live on the sea bed. They move around on tube feet, which have suckers on the ends.

▷ These **jelly-like animals** live in the sea. They have stinging tentacles for catching food and for protection.

Portuguese man-of-war

sea anemone

snail

▷ **Soft-bodied animals** need to keep their bodies moist, so many of them live in water. Some of them have a hard shell to protect their soft bodies.

octopus

Find out more

Amphibians
Birds
Camouflage
Conservation
Dinosaurs
Fish
Insects
Mammals
Prehistoric life
Reptiles
Spiders
Zoo

Antarctica and Arctic

The Antarctic and Arctic are very cold places. They are found at opposite ends of the Earth. Antarctica is in the south. It is the fifth biggest continent and is completely covered by ice. It is the coldest place on Earth. The Arctic is in the north. Most of it is a frozen ocean. In spring, some of its ice breaks up.

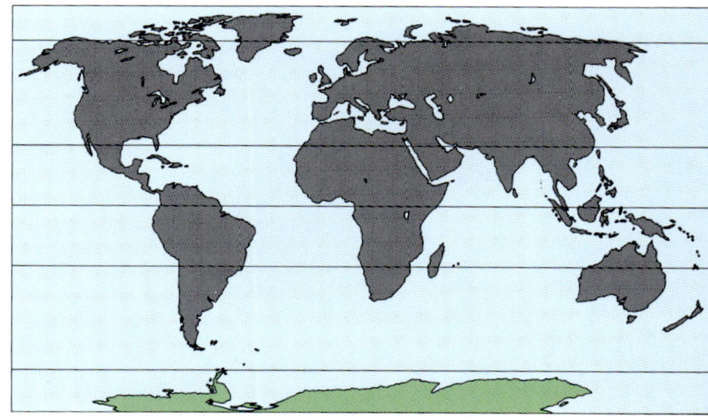

△ The Antarctic is shown in green and the Arctic is right at the top. They are the Earth's coldest places.

▷ Roald Amundsen, a Norwegian explorer, and his team were the first people to reach the South Pole, the centre of the Antarctic.

penguin

▽ Emperor penguins live in Antarctica. They hold their eggs and chicks on their feet to keep them warm.

polar bear

△ The polar bear lives in the Arctic. It is a strong swimmer and good runner. It catches seals, fish and birds with its strong paws and sharp claws.

△ Bands of coloured light can be seen in the skies of the Antarctic and Arctic. In the Arctic they are called the northern lights and in the Antarctic, the southern lights.

△ During the winter in the Arctic and Antarctic it is dark for up to 24 hours a day. In the summer, the opposite happens and the sun shines all night and day.

△ Many scientists work in the Arctic and Antarctic. They record the weather, measure the depth of the ice and study the wildlife.

Find out more
World

Art and artists

Art is something beautiful made by a person. Painting, carving, pottery and weaving are a few of the different types of art. Artists make works of art for all sorts of reasons. They may want to tell a story or record a place, a person or a special event. Sometimes artists can create things for a magical or religious reason, or just for pleasure.

△ The Aborigines of Australia painted rock or cave pictures thousands of years ago.

◁ The Ancient Greeks painted scenes from everyday life on their pottery vases. This man is hunting deer.

▷ Art is part of everyday life in Africa. People in Ghana weave colourful cloth with bold patterns for their clothes.

▷ This beautiful print of a stormy sea was made by a Japanese artist, called Hokusai. Scenes from nature are popular art subjects in Japan.

▽ This Polynesian sculptor is carving a stone figure called a tiki. He uses a hammer and sharp chisel to carve out the image.

▷ Edgar Degas, a French painter, painted many pictures of ballet dancers. He was interested in movement.

◁ Jackson Pollock, an American artist, laid his canvases on the floor and dripped, threw or poured paint all over them. The paint made swirling shapes and patterns.

Find out more

Africa
Books
Colour
Stories

Asia

Asia is the biggest continent. It has many kinds of land. There are large forests, deserts and grasslands. It has many high mountains and some very long rivers. More than half the world's people live in Asia. Many live in large, busy cities. Very few people live in the deserts or the rocky mountain areas.

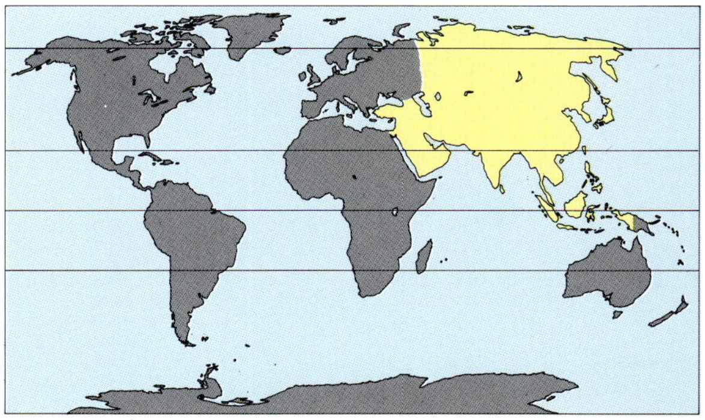

△ Asia is shown in yellow on this map. It covers nearly one third of all the land on the Earth.

△ Rice is grown in the warm, wet parts of Asia. Here it is grown in fields cut into the mountainside. The low-walled fields are flooded with water.

▽ Camels are raced in the desert country of Saudi Arabia. Camels carry goods across the desert. They can travel for days without drinking.

◁ Kyrgyz girls and women wear colourful clothes everyday. Kyrgyzstan is in northern Asia. The people herd sheep in winter and farm in summer.

◁ Shanghai, in China, is a very busy, crowded city. It is also the biggest city in China. New skyscrapers are being built to provide homes.

△ The tea ceremony is a very old and popular ceremony in Japan. The tea is made and drunk very slowly and carefully.

◁ The highest mountains in the world are in the Himalayas, between India and China. The highest of all is Mount Everest.

▽ Every July, at full moon, richly decorated elephants parade with dancers and drummers through the streets of Kandy in Sri Lanka.

Find out more

Dance
Drama
Farming
Religion
World

Australia and the Pacific Islands

Australia is the smallest continent and it is also a country. It is hot. Most people live in cities on the coast. Away from the coasts the land is called the bush and the outback. The Pacific is the world's largest and deepest ocean. It has many small islands. The Pacific islands, Australia and New Zealand together make up Oceania.

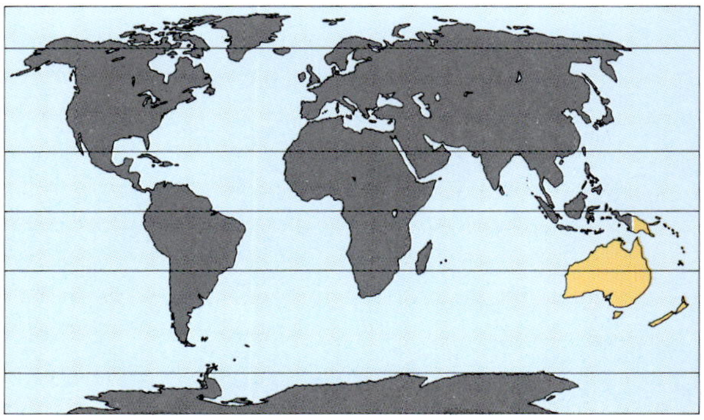

△ Australia, New Zealand and the many islands of the Pacific Ocean are shown in orange on this map.

△ A sheep shearer clips off a sheep's wool. Huge sheep stations cover large parts of Australia and New Zealand.

▽ Many Pacific islands are surrounded by coral reefs. Many kinds of brightly coloured fish live in the warm waters of the reef.

▷ These didgeridoo-players are Aborigines. Their ancestors were the first people to settle in Australia, a long time ago.

▷ Sydney is the largest city in Australia. It is also Australia's oldest city. Its world-famous Opera House (on the left of this picture) overlooks the harbour.

Uluru (Ayers Rock)

▷ The koala lives among the branches of eucalyptus trees. It feeds at night and sleeps all day. Its strong claws and special fingers help it cling to tree trunks.

koala bear

▽ On the North Island of New Zealand there are many geysers, which are jets of boiling water that burst into the air.

Find out more

- Buildings
- Farming
- History
- Stories
- World

Babies

Very young children are called babies. A baby begins when a tiny egg inside its mother joins together with a tiny part of its father called a sperm. The baby grows inside its mother's womb where it is kept safe and warm. After about nine months, the baby is ready to be born.

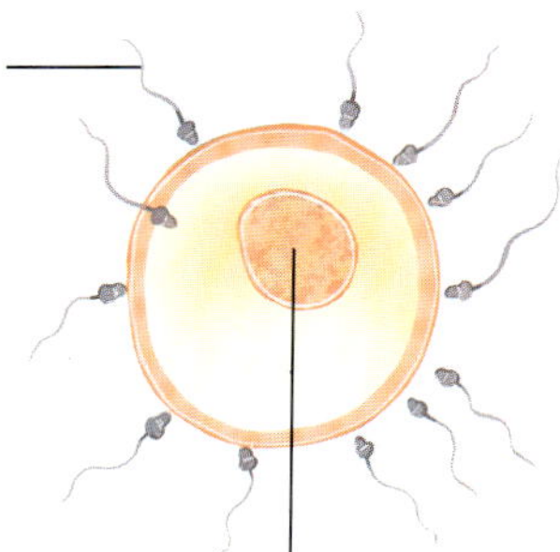

◁ This egg is surrounded by lots of sperm. Only one of the sperm will get inside the egg.

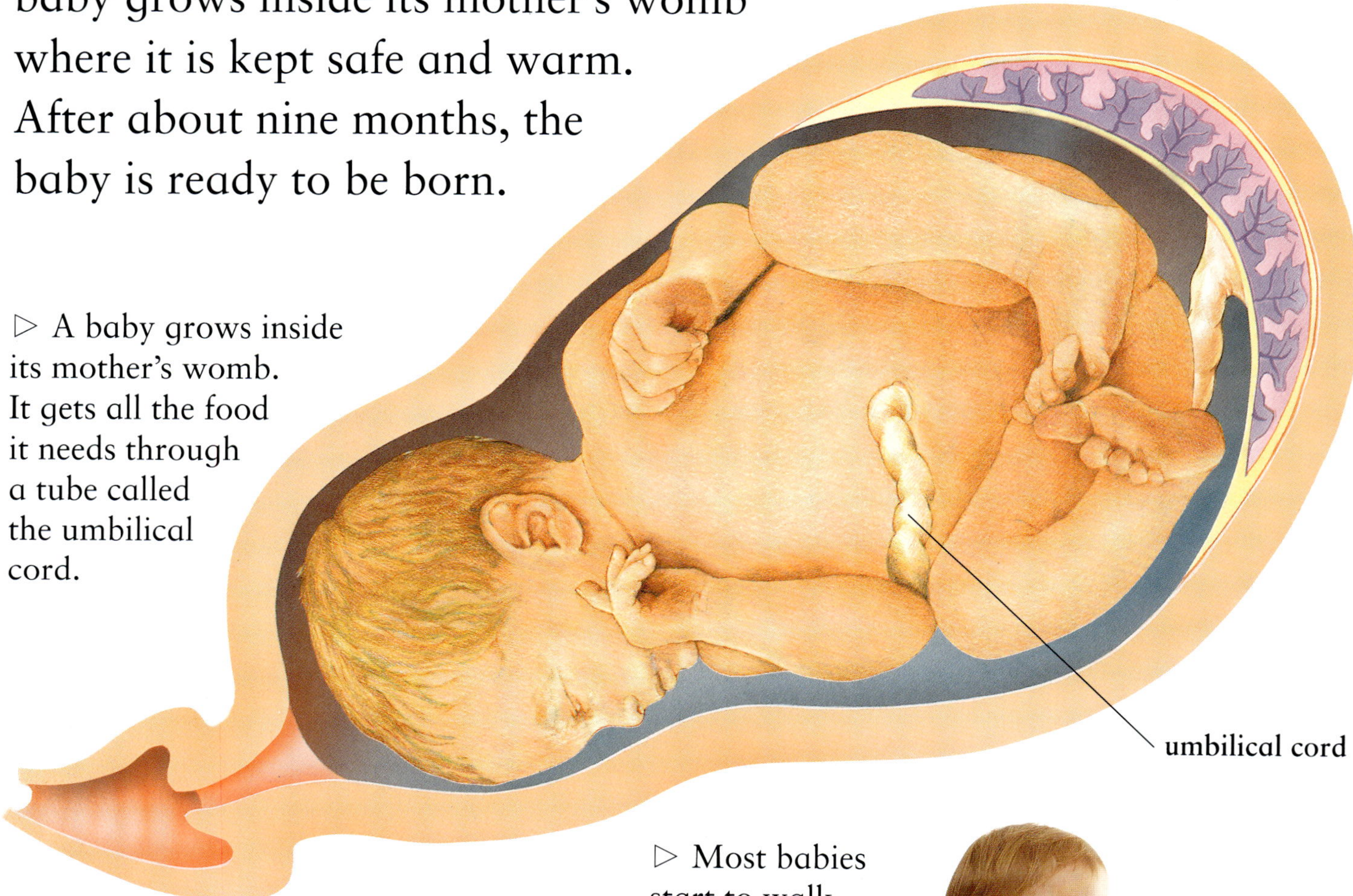

▷ A baby grows inside its mother's womb. It gets all the food it needs through a tube called the umbilical cord.

▽ A new born baby needs a lot of care and attention. It must be fed, bathed, kept warm and protected.

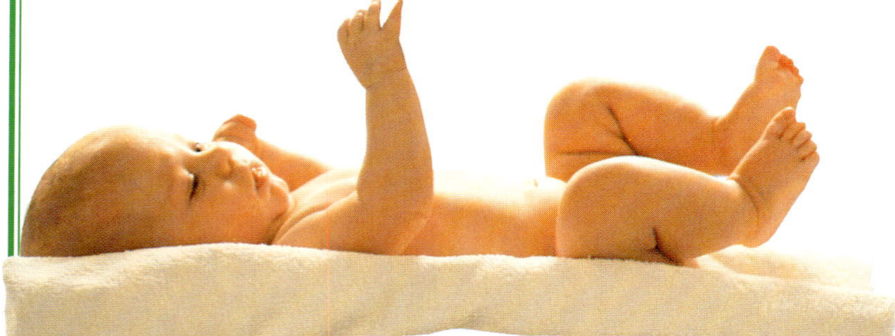

▷ Most babies start to walk without help between the ages of 12 and 18 months.

Find out more

Food
Human body
Mammals

Bikes

Bicycles, or bikes, are two-wheeled machines used to travel around. On a bike you can go from place to place much faster than you can walk. Motorbikes have engines and they can travel as fast as cars. Pedal bikes are a cheap, quiet and clean way to get around.

◁ This wooden bike was built over a hundred years ago.

△ The engine of a motorbike makes the wheels go round. The engine runs on petrol, which is stored in the fuel tank.

▽ To ride a bike you push the pedals. The pedals turn the chain. The chain moves the back wheel round. This makes the bike move.

Find out more
Energy
Inventions
Machines

Birds

Birds are the only animals with feathers. They also have wings. There are thousands of different birds, of all shapes, sizes and colours. The biggest bird in the world is an ostrich. The smallest bird is the tiny bee hummingbird, which is about the size of an ostrich's eye.

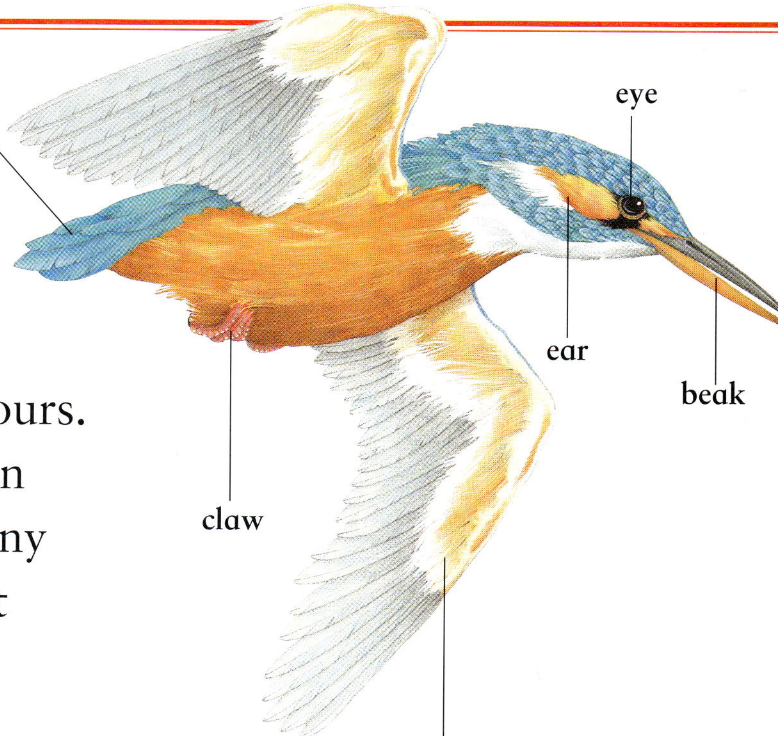

▷ Many male birds have colourful feathers to attract a female bird. A peacock shows off to a peahen.

peacock

▽ An ostrich has wings, but it is too heavy to fly. It uses its strong legs to run quickly. An ostrich can run faster than a racehorse.

▽ Most birds build nests for their eggs. When the chicks hatch the adult birds feed them. They are fed until they can leave the nest to find food.

herring gull

ostrich

wren

▷ A wren's beak is shaped for snapping up insects. An avocet has a long, curved beak to scoop up small water animals. A toucan uses its big beak to push aside leaves to pick fruit and nuts.

avocet

toucan

▽ Some birds are hunters. The powerful eagle uses its sharp, hooked talons to catch its prey.

eagle

Fact box

- Birds have beaks, or bills, instead of teeth.
- All birds hatch from eggs. The eggs have hard shells and are laid by the female bird.
- Most birds can fly. Penguins are birds that cannot fly. They use their wings to swim.
- Many birds have some hollow bones that help to make them light enough to fly.

Canada geese

▷ In autumn, many birds migrate. This means they fly away to warmer places where they can find food more easily.

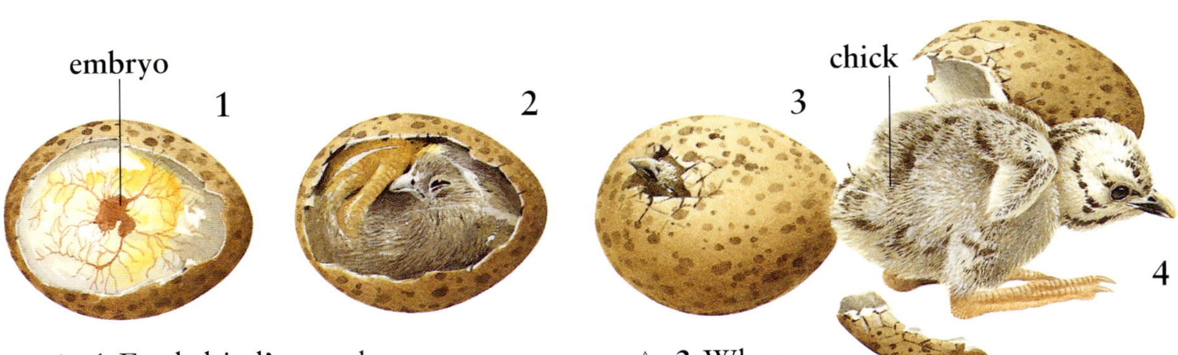

△ **1** Each bird's egg has an embryo. This is the part that can grow into a chick. **2** The chick grows bigger and bigger.

△ **3** When the chick is ready to hatch, it chips a hole in the eggshell. **4** Then the chick breaks out of the shell.

Find out more

Air
Animals
Antarctica and Arctic
Conservation
Prehistoric life
Seashore

Books

The first books were rare and precious. They were written by hand, which took a long time. Then a machine called a printing press was invented. This made it possible to make many copies of each book. Today most books are made of paper and cardboard. They are printed in enormous numbers on fast machines.

scrolls

◁ The Ancient Egyptians made some of the first books. They were written on scrolls.

▷ Long ago monks copied books by hand. They decorated each page with patterns and pictures.

▽ This printing machine was built by Johannes Gutenberg, over 500 years ago. The Bible was one of the first books he printed.

How a book is made

1

△ A team of people meet to plan the book. They decide on its size and what it will look like. They also choose an author to write it.

2

△ When the author has written the words, an editor carefully reads them. The editor corrects any mistakes on a computer screen.

3

△ An illustrator draws pictures to go with the words. Sometimes a photographer takes photographs to put in the book too.

4

△ The designer decides how to arrange the words and pictures on each page. She then puts the pages on to a computer disk.

5

△ From the disk, film and printing plates are made. At the printers a printing press prints the pages on to large sheets of paper.

6

△ The printed sheets are folded and cut into separate pages. They are stitched or glued together. Then a cover is put around the pages.

▷ You can use books to find out facts about animals, machines, history or science. Other books have stories in them. Millions of books are made every year.

Find out more

Forests
History
Maps
Stories
Writing

Buildings

Buildings give us shelter in all sorts of weather. Houses are often made of whatever materials can be found easily and most cheaply. They are built in all sorts of sizes and styles. Some buildings are built for a special purpose, such as offices, factories, sports centres and cinemas. Can you think of any others?

△ Log cabins were often built near forests. They had stone chimneys to protect the house from the fire.

△ Stone is very heavy. Stone houses were usually built in areas where the stone could be found nearby.

▽ Bundles of reeds were used to build houses in the marshes of Iraq. Reed houses were still built by Marsh Arabs until recently.

▽ In hot places, such as Africa, buildings are sometimes made of mud, baked by the sun. These are cool and shady.

△ Many houses are made of bricks. The bricks are joined with mortar, a mixture of water, sand and cement.

Famous Buildings

Leaning Tower of Pisa

Sydney Opera House

◁ Sydney Opera House, Australia overlooks a large harbour. Its roof looks like the sails of a boat.

◁ Italy's Leaning Tower of Pisa was built on soft ground. Every year the tower leans a tiny bit more.

▷ The Epcot Center at Disney World in Florida, USA, looks like a giant golf ball.

Epcot Center

◁ Skyscrapers have a skeleton made of steel. The walls are made of glass panels and thin concrete sheets.

Find out more

Australia and the Pacific Islands

Castles

Religion

Sport

Camouflage

The colours and markings of some animals match their surroundings. This makes them difficult to spot and is known as camouflage. Animals use camouflage to hide from their enemies. They can also creep up on the animals they are hunting without being seen.

leaf insect

◁ This strange leaf insect has markings on its wings that look just like the veins of a leaf.

tiger

◁ A tiger's coat has a pattern of dark and light stripes. This makes it hard to spot when it creeps through long grass.

Arctic hare

△ Arctic hares are white to match the snow in winter. In the summer, their fur turns brown.

△ A crafty chameleon can change the colour of its skin. This means it can hide in lots of different places.

▷ Camouflage material is made to help people hide. Bird-watchers can see much more if the birds cannot spot them.

Find out more

Forests

Grasslands

Cars

People drive all kinds of cars. There are family cars, racing cars, police cars, taxis, cross-country cars and long cars, called stretch-limousines. Most cars are powered by engines that need fuel to make them go. A few cars run on gas or electricity. Some even use energy from sunlight.

△ The first petrol-driven car was invented by a German, Karl Benz. He put an engine into a horse cart.

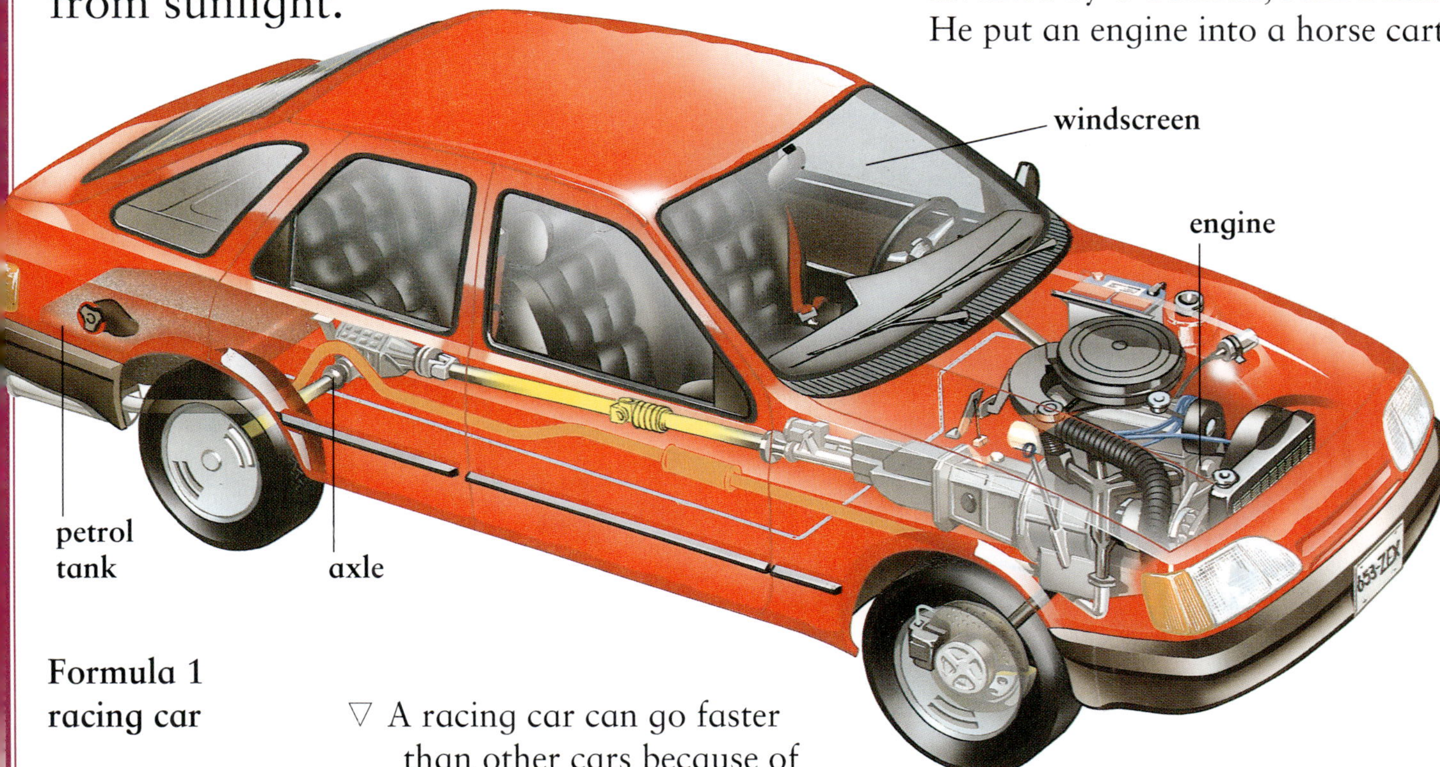

△ A car has hundreds of different moving parts to make it go.

Formula 1 racing car

▽ A racing car can go faster than other cars because of its powerful engine and wide wheels.

Jeep

▷ A Jeep is specially built to be driven over very bumpy ground. It also travels easily across deep mud and ice.

Find out more
Computers
Conservation
Energy
Inventions
Machines
Roads

Castles

Most castles were built hundreds of years ago. They had high towers and thick walls that sheltered people from their enemies. The first castles were built of wood. Later they were built of stone. Castles often have deep ditches around them called moats.

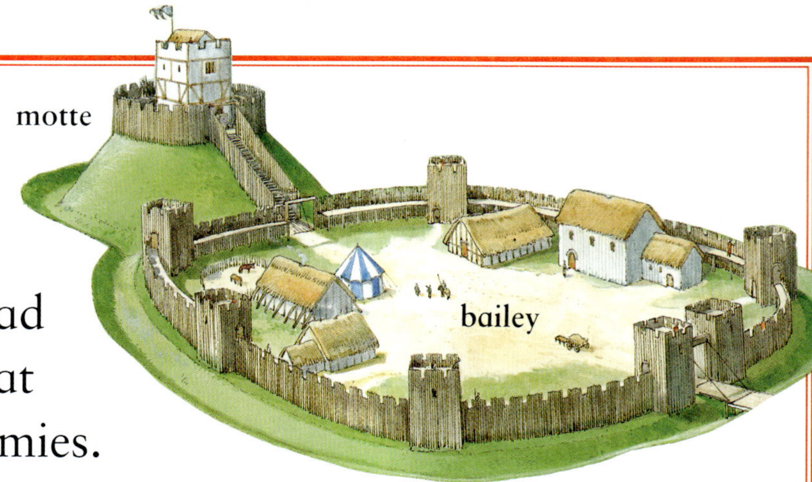

△ Wooden castles were built on a mound called a motte. People lived in an area outside the castle called a bailey. They only went into the castle when they were attacked.

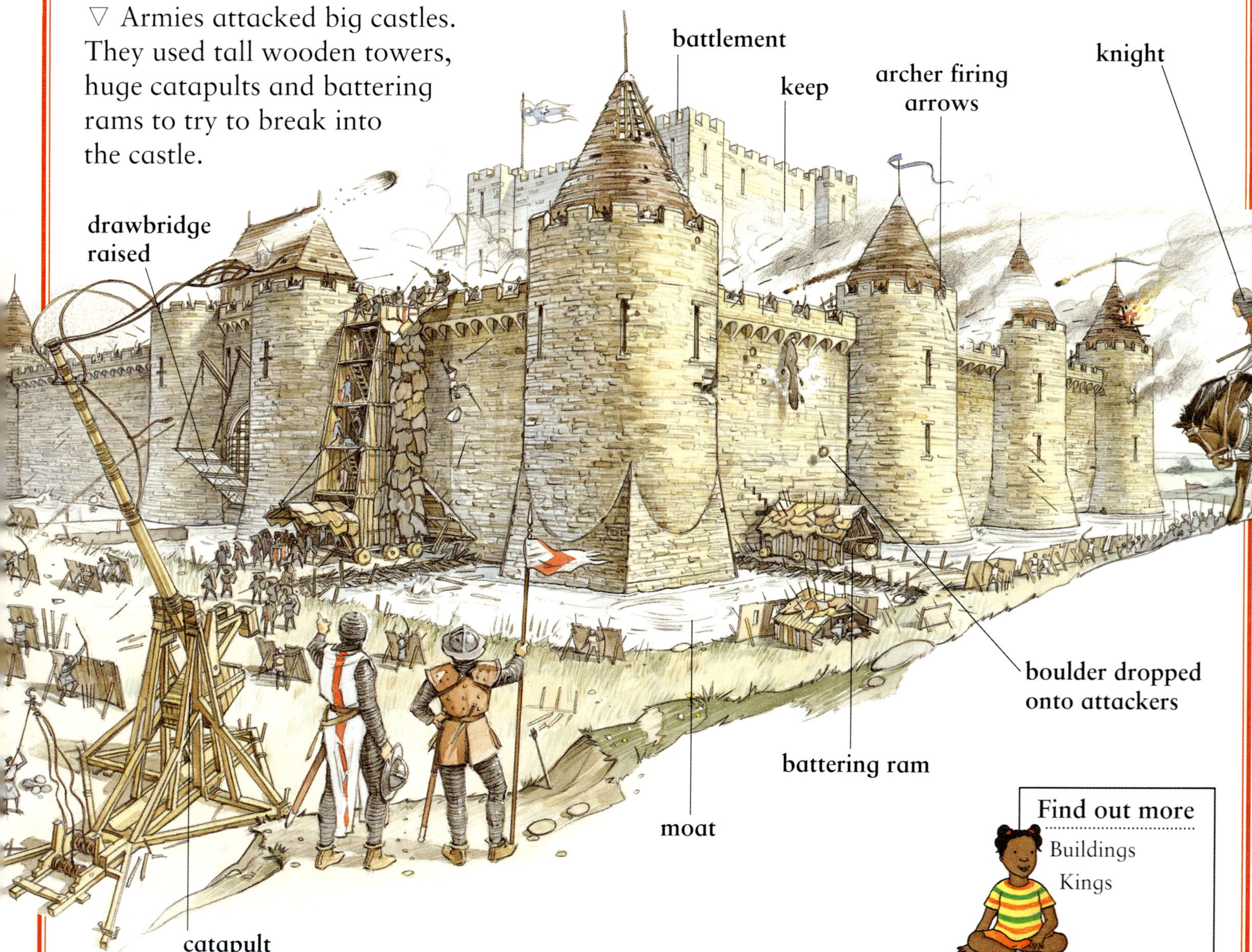

▽ Armies attacked big castles. They used tall wooden towers, huge catapults and battering rams to try to break into the castle.

Find out more
Buildings
Kings

Caves

Caves are big holes in rock. They are usually underground and are dark and damp. Most underground caves are found in rock called limestone. Rainwater and rivers can eat away limestone rocks. Sea water also crashes on to cliffs and hollows out caves. Caves can be used for shelter too.

△ Bats often live in caves. They sleep in them during the day and fly out to hunt after dark. The caves are a safe place for their young.

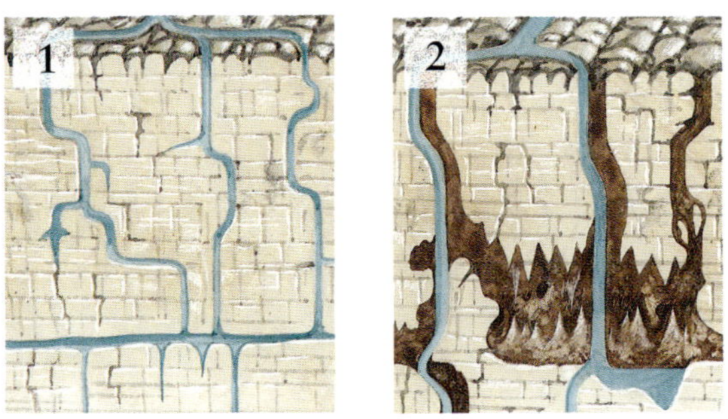

△ Water sinks into the cracks in limestone. It eats away at the rock to make tunnels.

△ Over thousands of years the tunnels get deeper and wider until they make big caves.

▷ Water dripping from the cave roof has minerals in it. When the water dries the minerals are left behind. They make stalactites, stalagmites and pillars.

Find out more

Art
Water

Clothes

All the things we wear are called clothes. People wear different clothes to suit the jobs they do, the games they play and the weather. In some jobs people wear uniforms so that they are easy to recognise. Most of the clothes we wear are made in factories.

Inuit child

◁ People that live in very cold places wear clothes that will keep them warm and dry.

Tuareg man

▷ In hot, dry deserts people wear long robes and scarves. They protect them from the heat of the Sun.

▽ When the weather is wet and rainy, you wear waterproof things to keep your clothes dry.

▽ Fire-fighters wear special clothes to protect them from the heat and the smoke.

fire-fighter

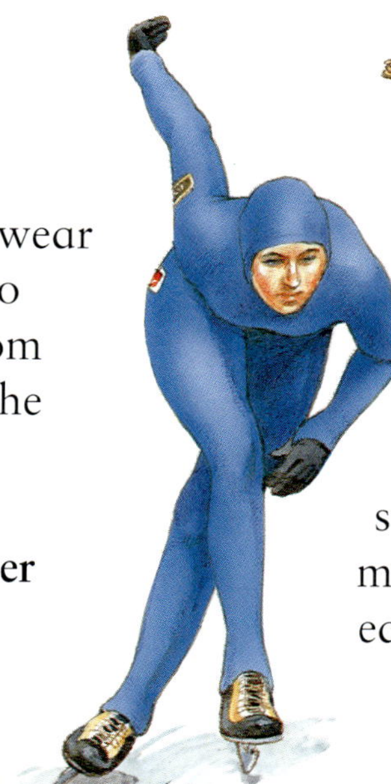

speed skater

◁ Clothes for sport are often tight and stretchy. They must be light and easy to move in.

Find out more
Dance
Desert
Drama
Space exploration
Sports

Colour

Our world is full of colours. Without them, it would be a very dull place. Colours are very useful. Plants grow bright flowers to attract insects. We use red signs to warn people of danger.

You need light to see colours. During the day you see lots of colours. At night, with no light, everything is black.

wasp

◁ A wasp has bright yellow stripes. These warn birds to keep away from its painful sting.

▷ Dyes are used to change the colour of fabrics. You can make dyes from natural things like plants, vegetables and berries.

△ Red, yellow and blue are the primary colours of paint. This means that they can be mixed together to make almost any other colour, apart from white.

▽ Red, blue and green are the primary colours of light. They can be mixed in different amounts to make other colours. An equal mix of red, blue and green makes white light.

Find out more
Art and artists
Camouflage
Light

Computers

A computer is a machine that can store and find huge amounts of information and solve difficult number problems very fast. Banks, shops, factories and offices all use computers. Computers are also used at home. Computers contain parts, called microchips, to make them work. They use programs to tell them what to do.

△ The Colossus, one of the earliest computers, was enormous. It helped to decode enemy messages during World War II.

△ Car factories use computer-controlled robots to build cars. The robots weld the car parts together.

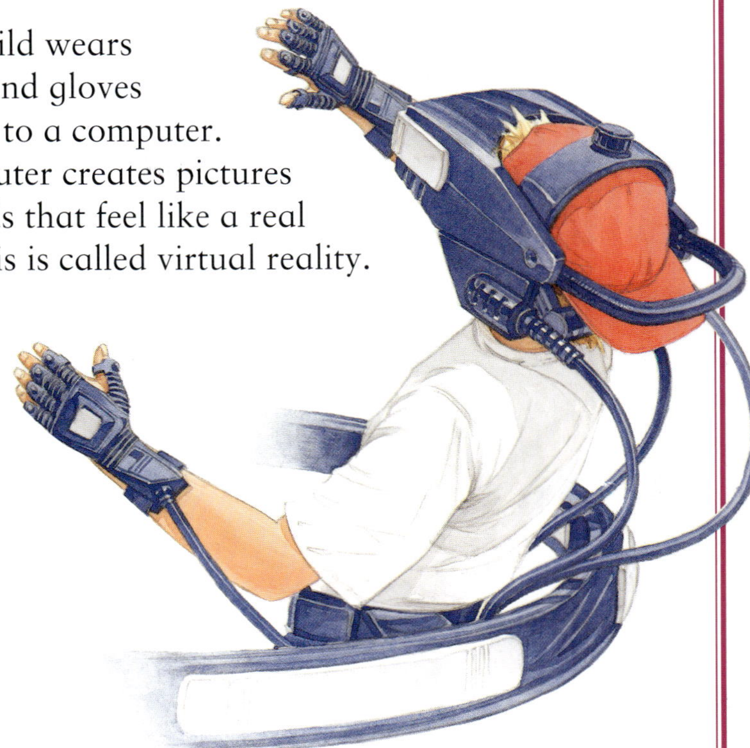

▷ This child wears a helmet and gloves connected to a computer. The computer creates pictures and sounds that feel like a real world. This is called virtual reality.

2 You can enter information into a computer using a keyboard and a mouse, a floppy disk or a CD-ROM. You can also search for information on the internet. Words and pictures show up on a screen called a monitor.

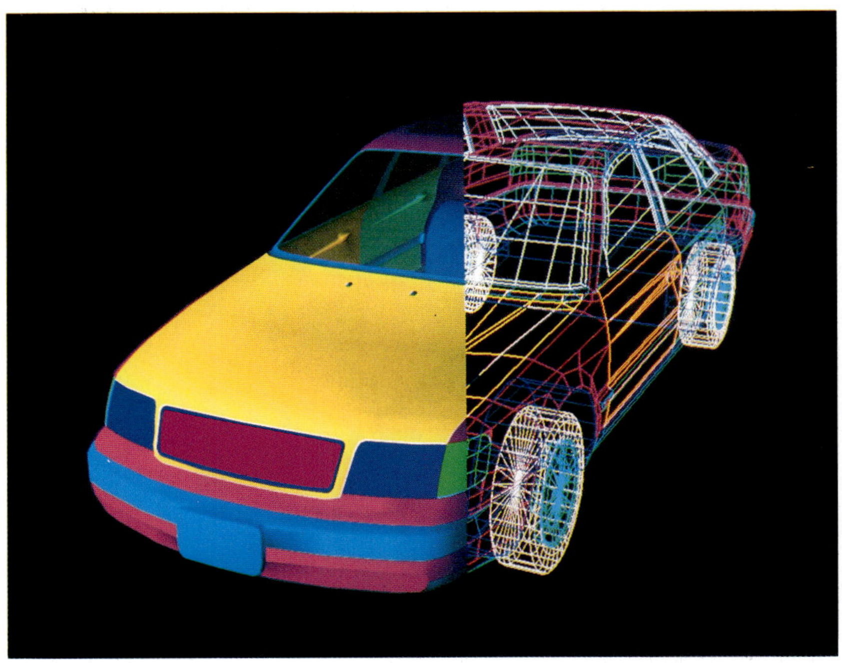

△ Car designers use computers to draw new cars. The computer can test out the designs to see if the new car will work on the road.

◁ Computers can be used for fun. You have to be quick to score well on a handheld computer game.

Find out more

Books
Electricity
Jobs
Music
Space exploration

Conservation

Conservation is the protection of our world and its wildlife. This is hard to do because people can destroy the places where animals and plants live. People also hunt animals for their fur, horns and meat. Some animals and plants have become extinct, which means that they have died out.

dodo

◁ This bird is called a dodo. It became extinct nearly 200 years ago.

rhinoceros

◁ If hunters go on killing rare rhinos for their horns they will die out.

slipper orchid

▷ Some wild orchids are very rare, but people still dig them up.

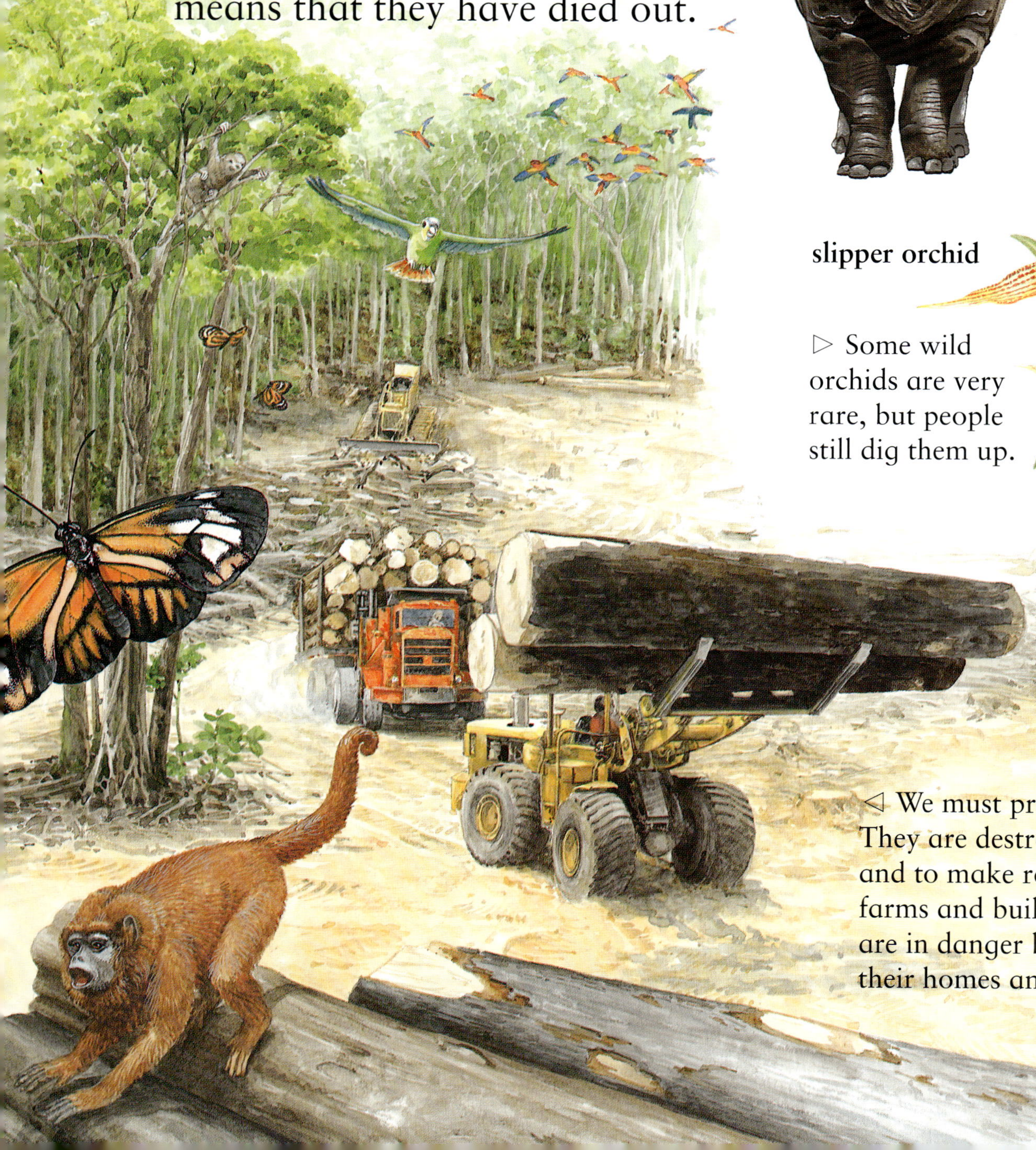

◁ We must protect our forests. They are destroyed for timber and to make room for roads, farms and buildings. Animals are in danger because they lose their homes and their food.

△ Waste pumped out by factories can poison the air and water. This is called pollution.

△ Chemicals that farmers spray on crops to make them grow can harm wild plants and animals.

△ Some cars let out fumes that pollute the air and the soil. These kill plants and can make people ill.

▷ A bird covered in oil spilt by a tanker will die unless it is carefully washed.

▷ If you plant a tree, it will soon become a home for many different creatures.

▷ You can help clean up your world by saving card, paper, bottles and tins to be used again. This is called recycling.

Find out more

Energy
Farming
Forests
Plants
Zoo

Dance

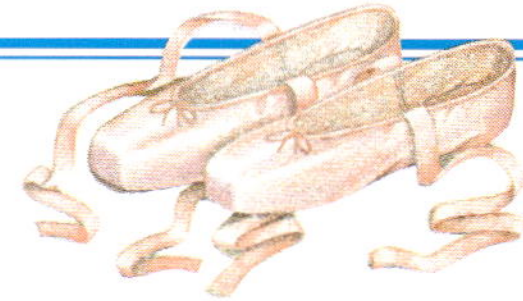

ballet shoes

When you dance, you move your body in time to music. You may follow a pattern of steps, or just twist and twirl and stamp your feet to fit the music. People all over the world love to dance. Many dancers tell a story with their hands and bodies instead of words.

◁ This Indian dancer moves her hands and fingers in a special way to tell a story about Hindu gods.

▷ Most ballet dancers first learn to dance when they are very young. They learn special positions for their hands and feet.

◁ Spanish flamenco dancers stamp and tap their heels and toes. They move their hands, while twisting and turning their bodies in time to guitar music.

▷ These Russian folk dancers leap up high and kick out their legs to fast music.

Find out more

Art and artists
Asia
Europe
Music
Religion

Desert

A desert is a dry place where little or no rain falls. Few people live there. Only tough plants and animals can live in these rocky or sandy places. Some deserts are blazing hot during the day and freezing cold at night. Other deserts are cold most of the time.

△ Monument Valley is in North America. Sand is blown about by strong winds and this has worn the rocks into these strange shapes.

▷ These people are nomads. This means that they move around to find food and water. They often live in tents that can be moved easily.

desert scorpion

△ The scorpion is a deadly hunter. It has a poisonous sting in its tail.

camel

◁ A camel can travel a long way without food and water. It lives on fat which is stored in its hump.

prickly pear cactus

◁ Cactus plants store water in their thick stems. The spines protect them from being eaten by animals.

Find out more

Africa
Antarctica and Arctic
Asia
North America
Plants

Dinosaurs

Dinosaurs lived on Earth millions of years ago. These scaly-skinned reptiles were all shapes and sizes. There were huge creatures that weighed ten times as much as an elephant, and others the size of chickens. Some were fierce meat-eaters and some only ate plants.

△ Scientists study fossils of dinosaur footprints. They can use them to work out how they moved and how fast they ran.

Fact box

- The word dinosaur means terrible lizard.
- Dinosaurs lived on Earth long before the first human beings.
- Dinosaurs became extinct about 65 million years ago. We do not know why they died out.

◁ Dinosaurs laid eggs just like reptiles do today. Maiasaura laid eggs in a nest. This dinosaur cared for her babies after they hatched.

Maiasaura
(**My**-a-**saw**-ra)

▷ You can visit a museum to find out about dinosaurs. This is the skeleton of Tyrannosaurus rex. Scientists have studied its bones and teeth to find out how it lived.

▷ For a long time scientists thought that Tyrannosaurus rex was the biggest meat-eating dinosaur. Then they discovered an even bigger meat-eater which they called Gigantosaurus.

Gigantosaurus
(Jie-**gant**-o-**saw**-rus)

Tyrannosaurus
(Tie-**ran**-o-**saw**-rus)

▷ The smallest dinosaur was Compsognathus. It was about the size of a chicken and ran very fast.

Compsognathus
(Komp-**sog**-nath-us)

▷ Deinonychus had razor-sharp claws. They hunted in packs so that they could attack much larger dinosaurs.

Deinonychus
(**Dine**-o-**nike**-us)

Stegosaurus
(**Steg**-o-**saw**-rus)

▷ Stegosaurus could not run to escape attack, so it had to defend itself. It had large, sharp plates along its back and long spikes on its tail.

Find out more
Fossils
Prehistoric life
Reptiles

Drama

Drama is a story told in words and actions. Most dramas are called plays. They are performed by actors on a stage in front of an audience. Most plays are performed in a theatre. You can also watch drama on the television and in the cinema, or listen to it on the radio.

◁ Puppets can be used instead of people to perform plays. These puppets are from India.

▷ You could put on your own play. Decide on a story and make some scenery. Dress up in costumes and put on make-up. Then ask people to come along and watch.

△ This woman is a mime artist. She uses her body to tell a story without words.

◁ Kabuki is a type of play performed in Japan. All the actors are men. They wear colourful costumes and lots of make-up.

Find out more
History
Jobs
Stories

Earth

The Earth is our planet. It is a giant ball of rock spinning in Space around the Sun. It is the only planet we know that has life. The Earth gets all the heat and light it needs from the Sun. A blanket of air, called the atmosphere, surrounds the Earth. This is the air we breathe. Large oceans of water cover most of the Earth's surface. Air and water are essential for life.

△ This is how the Earth looks from Space. Swirling, white patterns are made by clouds in the atmosphere.

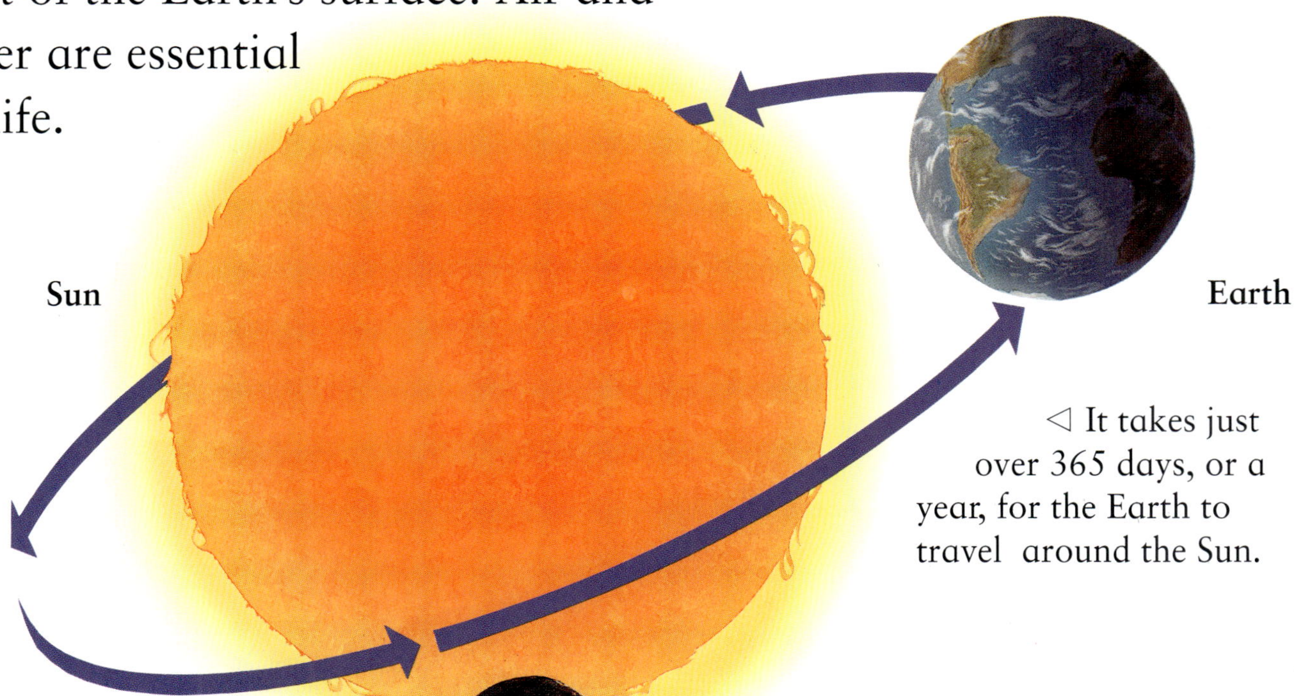

◁ It takes just over 365 days, or a year, for the Earth to travel around the Sun.

▷ We have day and night because the Earth turns as it travels around the Sun. Imagine the torch is the Sun. The side facing it has daylight. The other side has night.

The **crust** is the rocky surface of Earth beneath your feet.
The **mantle** is a thick layer of rock. Some of it is melted rock.
The **outer core** is made of hot, runny metal. It is very hot here.
The **inner core** is solid metal. It is the hottest place on Earth.

▽ The crust is made up of many different types of rock. Most are made deep inside the Earth.

sandstone

marble

limestone

granite

▷ Gems are rare crystals found in rocks. They are cut and polished to make jewels.

amethyst

yellow sapphire

rock crystal

Fact box

- Large oceans cover about three-quarters of the Earth.
- The Earth was formed about 4.6 billion years ago from clouds of hot gas and dust.
- Earth measures 40,075 km round its middle. If you walked day and night it would take over a year to walk round it.

△ Coal is made from the remains of plants that died millions of years ago. It is dug out of the ground by miners and used as fuel.

△ Miners drill for oil and gas on land and under the sea. They often work on huge rigs far out at sea.

▷ Earthquakes happen when parts of the crust push against each other or move apart. This makes the ground shake. Cracks appear in the ground and buildings may collapse.

Find out more

Oceans and seas
Planets
Seasons
Sun
Volcano
Weather
World

Electricity

Electricity is a type of energy. It moves along wires. When it flows along a wire this is called an electric current. Electricity is used to make heat, light, sound and movement - it can make all kinds of machines work. Electricity can be stored in batteries too.

△ You can make static electricity. Rub a balloon on a jumper. The static will make it stick to the wall.

Never play with, or go near, electrical sockets. Electricity can kill you.

▷ To light the bulb, electricity flows from the battery down the wire through the bulb and back to the battery. This is called a circuit.

◁ Electricity is important in our daily lives. None of these machines could work without it. They all use electricity.

Find out more

Cars
Energy
Light
Trains
Weather

Energy

Light, sound and heat are all forms of energy. Some forms of energy can make things move. You use energy when you run or jump. Energy can move from place to place, but it is usually carried by something. Sound is carried by the air and electricity by wires. Energy to light and heat our homes is made by burning coal, oil or gas, but some can be made by wind and water.

△ You can use your energy to make things happen. This girl is using her energy to blow. This makes the sails of the windmill spin around.

▷ The Sun provides the energy for trees and plants.

△ Plants use the Sun's heat and light to grow. Cows eat the grass.

△ Cows use the energy from the grass to make milk.

◁ This energy helps us to walk, run, jump and talk.

◁ When you drink milk or eat food it gives your body lots of energy.

△ Energy never disappears, but it can be stored. When you push back on a swing you are storing some energy.

△ When you let go, the energy changes from stored energy to movement energy and you move forward.

oil

coal

gas

◁ The Sun's energy is stored in oil, coal and gas. These were made millions of years ago from dead plants. We burn them to make electricity.

△ Petrol is made from oil. Cars burn petrol to give out its energy. This energy makes the car move.

▷ Burning petrol and diesel can cause pollution. This is mainly produced by the exhaust fumes from cars, lorries, buses and motorbikes.

▽ The silver solar panels all over this car use light direct from the Sun to power the car and make the wheels turn.

solar-powered car

△ Energy made from water is called hydroelectric power. The water is stored behind a dam. As it flows down a pipe it creates electricity by driving a generator.

◁ Windmills on a wind farm can also be used to make electricity. Solar power, water and wind energy do not cause pollution.

Find out more

Cars
Earth
Electricity
Food
Health
Light
Sun

Europe

Europe is the second smallest continent – only Australia is smaller. It stretches from the snowy Arctic in the north to the warm lands of the Mediterranean Sea in the south. It has high mountains, large forests and many rivers. Many people live in Europe and some parts are very crowded. Most people live in or near cities.

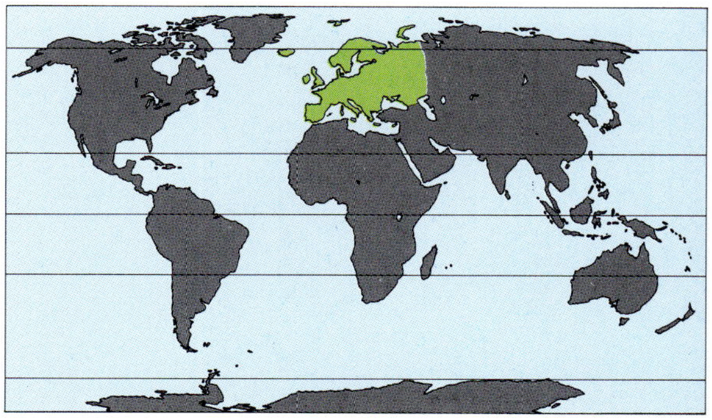

△ Europe is shown in green on this map. Europe has a ragged outline. In the east it is joined to Asia.

◁ The peacock butterfly is found in gardens, woods and mountains all over Europe, except in the cold north.

peacock butterfly

▽ St Basil's Cathedral is in Moscow, the capital city of Russia. Russia is the largest country in the world. It stretches across Europe and Asia.

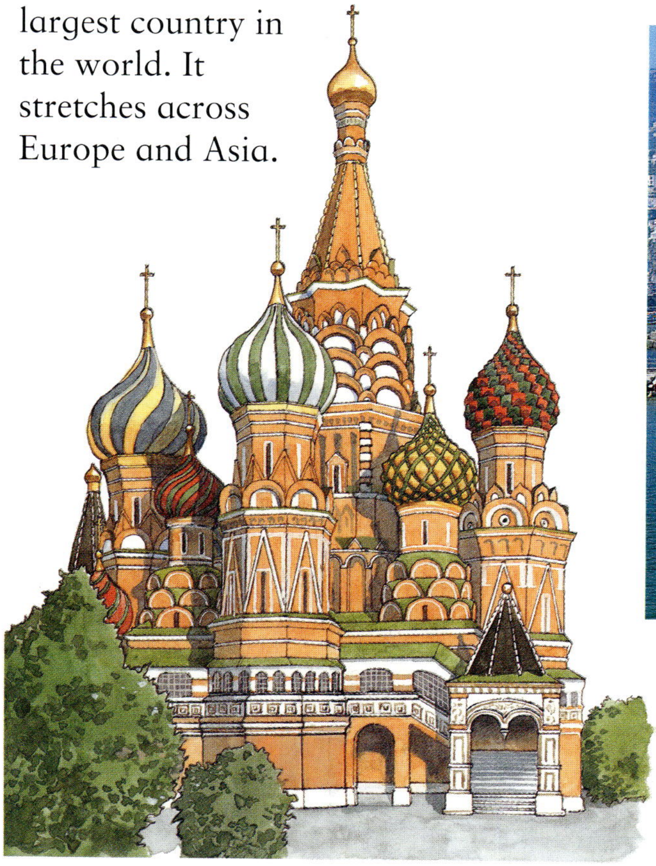

△ A beach in Amalfi, Italy in southern Europe. Millions of tourists come to enjoy a holiday in the warm waters around the Mediterranean Sea.

◁ In Sweden, people dance around a maypole on Midsummer's Eve to mark the return of summer.

▽ Along the coast of Norway, in northern Europe, there are deep inlets of sea with steep sides, called fjords.

▷ Olive trees grow in rows on the hot, dry hills of southern Spain. Lots of Mediterranean countries grow olives and many other fruits.

◁ The Danube River flows through the middle of Budapest, the capital of Hungary. Like many European cities, Budapest has lots of fine old buildings in its centre.

Find out more

History
Maps
World

Farming

All over the world, farmers grow crops and raise animals for food. They plant fields of wheat, rice, corn, oats and vegetables. They raise animals for their meat, milk and eggs. Many farms use machines to do much of the work. Some farms do all the work by hand.

▽ Rice is an important crop in China, India and other countries in Asia. It is grown in flooded fields called paddies. It is usually sown and picked by hand.

▷ Wheat is usually grown in huge fields. It is harvested by a combine harvester. Wheat grain is ground up into flour to make bread and pasta.

△ Milk from cows is used to make dairy produce such as cheese, butter and cream.

△ Female chickens are called hens. They lay eggs. People eat chickens' eggs and meat.

Fact box

- Farming began 10,000 years ago. Before then people survived by hunting animals and gathering plants.
- Two of the most widely eaten foods are rice and potatoes.
- Over half of the world's people eat rice at every meal.

◁ Large flocks of sheep are raised on sheep stations in New Zealand and Australia. Their wool is clipped off, cleaned and spun into yarn.

◁ Pests, such as the Colorado beetle, destroy crops. Farmers spray the crops with chemicals to kill the pests.

Colorado potato beetle

△ This tractor is spreading manure over a ploughed field. Manure is a fertilizer. It feeds the soil and helps new crops to grow large and strong.

Find out more

Asia

Australia and the Pacific Islands

Conservation

Europe

Fish

Fish live in water and are all different shapes and sizes. The enormous whale shark can be up to 15 metres long. A tiny fish called a pygmy goby is no longer than your fingernail. Some fish live in warm, shallow water. Others live in the cold, deep sea.

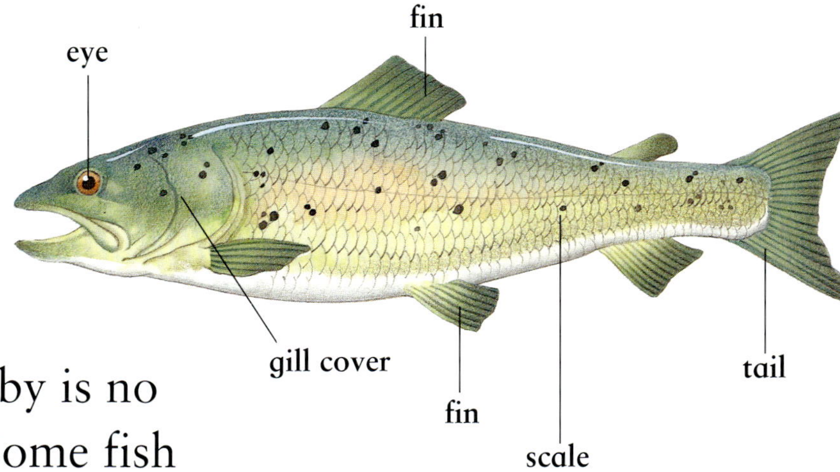

great white shark

◁ Great white sharks are fast swimmers and fierce hunters. They use their razor-sharp teeth to tear apart their prey.

▽ Blue marlin and many other big fish live far away from the shore. Tuna and mackerel live close to the surface. Sawfish and rays live on the sea bed.

puffer fish

▷ A puffer fish can blow up its body like a balloon. It does this to scare away its enemies.

African cichlid

▷ The babies of the African cichlid fish swim into their mother's mouth to escape from danger.

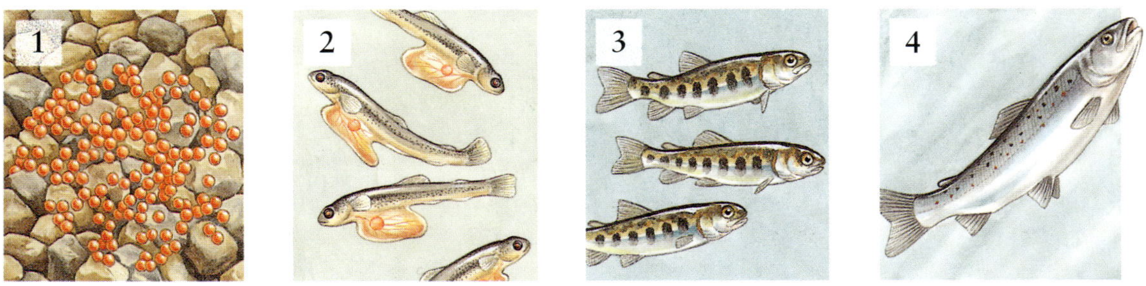

△ **1** A female salmon lays her eggs in a river. **2** When the eggs hatch, the babies are called fry.

△ **3** The young salmon live in the river for over two years. **4** Then they swim down to the sea.

Fact box

- A fish is a vertebrate, which means that it has a backbone.
- They breathe by taking in oxygen from the water through their gills.
- Most fish swim through the water by moving their tails from side to side.

▽ Fish that live in the warm, shallow water around coral reefs are often brightly coloured. Their bold patterns help them to hide among the corals and to creep up on their prey.

angel fish

Find out more

Animals
Fishing
Food
Oceans and seas
Prehistoric life
Water

Fishing

Rivers, seas and oceans are full of fish and other creatures that people like to eat. Every day people set off in their fishing boats to catch different types of fish. They often use trawler boats with huge nets that can scoop up thousands of fish at a time.

◁ A large net bag is dragged behind a stern trawler. It can catch fish on the sea bed.

stern trawler net

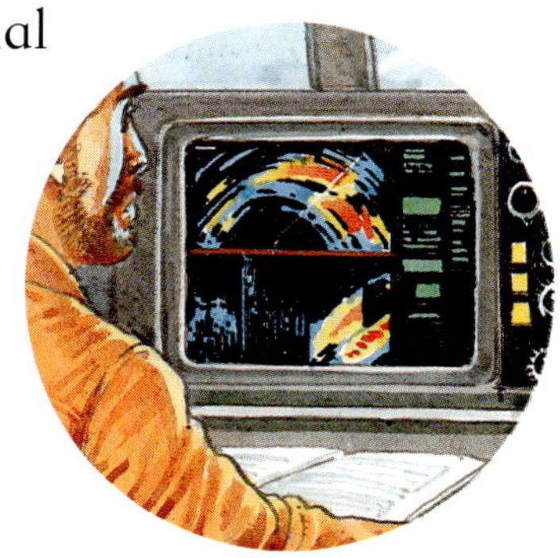

▷ Some fishing boats use special equipment called sonar to find shoals of fish.

▷ A purse seine net is towed around a shoal of fish. The net is gathered in by a huge rope.

purse seine net

▷ Long drift nets are used to trap fish that swim near the surface of the water.

drift net

◁ A net full of fish is hauled onto a trawler. The fish are sorted and cleaned. Then they are packed in ice to keep them fresh.

Find out more

Australia and the Pacific Islands
Fish
Oceans and seas
Ships and boats
Water

Flowers

Most plants have flowers. They are a very important part of a plant, because they make the seeds that grow into new plants. Many flowers have bright colours and a sweet smell to attract insects, such as bees and butterflies. The insects carry tiny grains of pollen from one flower to another so that seeds can be made.

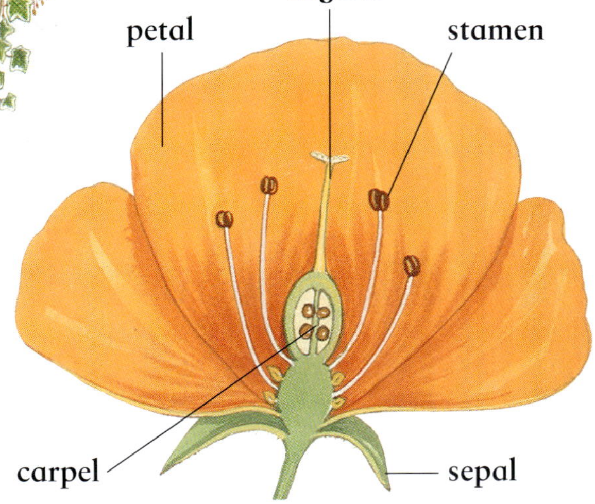

△ These are the parts of a flower. Pollen is carried from the stamen of one flower to the stigma of another. This is called pollination.

▷ Flowers make nectar, which bees like to drink. As the bee drinks, pollen sticks to its body. When it flies to another flower, the pollen rubs off and pollinates it.

◁ Some flowers are pollinated by the wind. Pollen is blown from the male catkins to the female catkins.

1 2 3 4

△ **1** The flowers of a pear tree are pollinated by insects. **2** Tiny fruits start to grow under the flowers. The fruit protects the seeds inside.

△ **3** The fruits swell and grow. **4** When the fruits are fully grown they soften. Animals eat the fruit and spread the seeds.

Find out more
Conservation
Insects
Plants
Seasons
Water

Flying machines

There are all kinds of different flying machines, from hot-air balloons and gliders, to helicopters and passenger planes. The fastest way to travel is by aeroplane. An aeroplane has wings to lift it up into the air and an engine to push it forward. For hundreds of years people dreamed of being able to fly like a bird, but not until the 20th century were they successful.

△ The first aeroplane was built by the Wright brothers over 100 years ago. The pilot had to lie on his stomach to fly it.

▷ This passenger jet can carry about 250 people. Jumbo jets are the largest passenger planes in the world. They can carry more than 400 people.

hot-air balloon

△ The air inside a hot-air balloon is heated by a powerful gas burner. Because hot air rises, it makes the balloon float up into the sky.

▽ This is a fighter plane. It is called a jump jet because it can take off straight up into the air. It can also hover above the ground.

jump jet

▷ A helicopter has whirling rotor blades instead of wings. It can fly up, down, sideways, backwards, forwards or hover in the air.

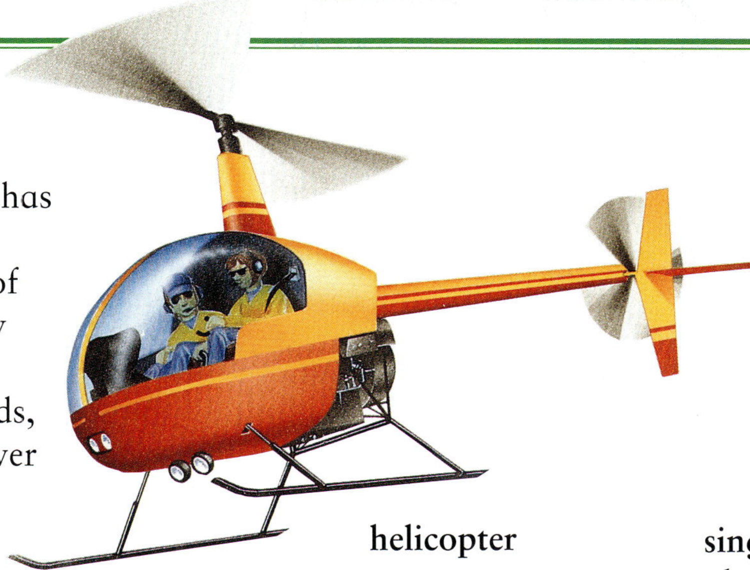

helicopter

▽ Some small, light aeroplanes have only one engine and are driven by a spinning propeller at the front.

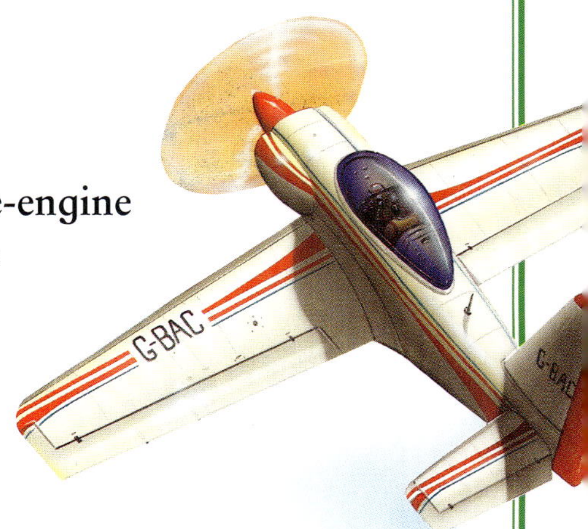

single-engine plane

passenger jet

The first flight powered by a human and not an engine was made in the *Gossamer Albatross*. Its pilot used bicycle pedals to turn a large propeller.

Gossamer Albatross

Find out more

Air

Space exploration

Food

Food is important because it gives you energy to move and keep warm. It helps you to grow and to get better when you are ill. To stay healthy you need to eat lots of different kinds of food. You also need plenty of water to drink. Eating too many sugary or fatty foods is bad for your body.

△ Cheese, meat, eggs, nuts and fish give you proteins that build up your body and help it to stay strong.

▷ Fruit and vegetables have plenty of fibre. They help the food that you eat to pass through your body.

△ Fats from foods like butter, milk, bacon, margarine and oil give you lots of energy. Your body can store extra fat to use later.

△ Carbohydrates also give your body energy. Foods like bread, pasta, potatoes, noodles, beans and rice all have carbohydrates in them.

▷ Vitamins are found in many different kinds of food. They help to keep your body working properly. Six kinds of vitamins are shown in this picture. There are about twenty different vitamins altogether.

▽ People eat many different kinds of food. The weather in different countries helps to decide which foods people grow.

Find out more

Asia
Energy
Farming
Fishing
Health
Human body
Water

Forests

Forests grow all over the world. The forest trees that grow in cold, dry parts of the world are very different from the trees that grow in warm, wet parts of the world.

A forest is home to many animals. The trees give them food and shelter them from the Sun, rain and wind.

△ Look at all these things. Wood from trees has been used to make them. Even the pages of this book are made from wood.

◁ Rainforests grow in hot, wet places. Over half of the world's animals and plants live in these forests. Huge areas of rainforest are cut down each year. This means that many of the animals and plants are in danger of dying out.

deciduous forests

◁ Deciduous forests are full of trees that lose their leaves in the autumn.

badger

△ The European badger lives in an underground home called a set. It hunts in the forest at night.

white-tailed deer

jay

△ The deer's spots make them hard to see in the forest. This is called camouflage.

◁ Jays eat the fruit from oak trees. They often bury the acorns, then dig them up when it is hard to find food in the winter.

coniferous forests

▷ Forests in cold places are full of coniferous trees. They keep their leaves all through the year.

moose

chipmunk

◁ A moose is a very large deer. It feeds on water plants and young tree shoots.

△ A chipmunk uses pouches in its cheeks to carry nuts and seeds back to its food store.

Find out more

Buildings
Conservation
Mountains
Trees
Trucks

Fossils

Fossils are the remains of plants and animals. Scientists study fossils of leaves, shells, footprints and skeletons to find out about life on Earth millions of years ago. When the plants and animals died, their remains were very slowly turned to stone.

▷ Nearly 200 years ago, 12-year-old Mary Anning found a huge fossil in a cliff. It was a sea creature called Plesiosaurus.

△ **1** Ammonites lived in the sea millions of years ago. **2** When one died, its soft body rotted away. Layers of mud buried its hard shell.

△ **3** Very slowly, over thousands of years, the mud turned to rock and the shell became a fossil. **4** Many years later the fossil was dug up.

spider in amber

△ This spider has been kept whole in a piece of amber. Amber is sticky tree sap which has turned hard.

▷ This Woolly mammoth was frozen for thousands of years in the icy ground of Siberia, in Russia.

Woolly mammoth

◁ Fossils of plants are often found in large lumps of coal. This is a type of fern.

Find out more
Dinosaurs
Prehistoric life

Grasslands

Grasslands cover huge areas of the world. They are sometimes too dry for many trees to grow. Grasses are tough plants that grow quickly.

The hot grassland of Africa is called savanna and in Australia it is called the bush. Grasslands are called pampas in South America, prairies in North America and steppes in Asia.

▽ The African savanna often looks brown and dry. In the short rainy season it is fresh and green.

△ In Australia the bush often catches fire in the dry season. Grass grows well in the ash-rich soil.

△ Huge areas of the prairies of North America are used to grow wheat.

pampas grass

◁ This type of grass grows on the pampas of South America. It has long, fluffy flowers.

Find out more

Africa
Asia
Camouflage
Farming
North America
South America

Health

You need to be healthy to keep your body working properly. A healthy diet gives your body fuel and helps it to grow and repair itself. Keeping clean helps to stop the germs that can cause illness spreading. Exercise helps your body to grow strong. Caring for yourself will keep you fit and healthy.

△ You need different foods to keep you strong and healthy. Eating a variety of foods and drinking lots of water gives you energy and helps you grow.

◁ Playing football and other games is a good way to take exercise. Exercise makes your muscles strong and keeps your body fit.

▽ Washing with soap and water keeps your skin clean. Keeping clean stops illnesses and germs spreading.

Fact box

- The outside of your teeth is covered with hard enamel. Fizzy drinks and sweets eat this away.
- People are given injections, called vaccinations, to prevent them catching nasty illnesses.
- Most children sleep for about 12 hours every night.

▷ If you graze your skin, it should be cleaned so that germs cannot get in. Germs are tiny living things. Some of them can make you ill.

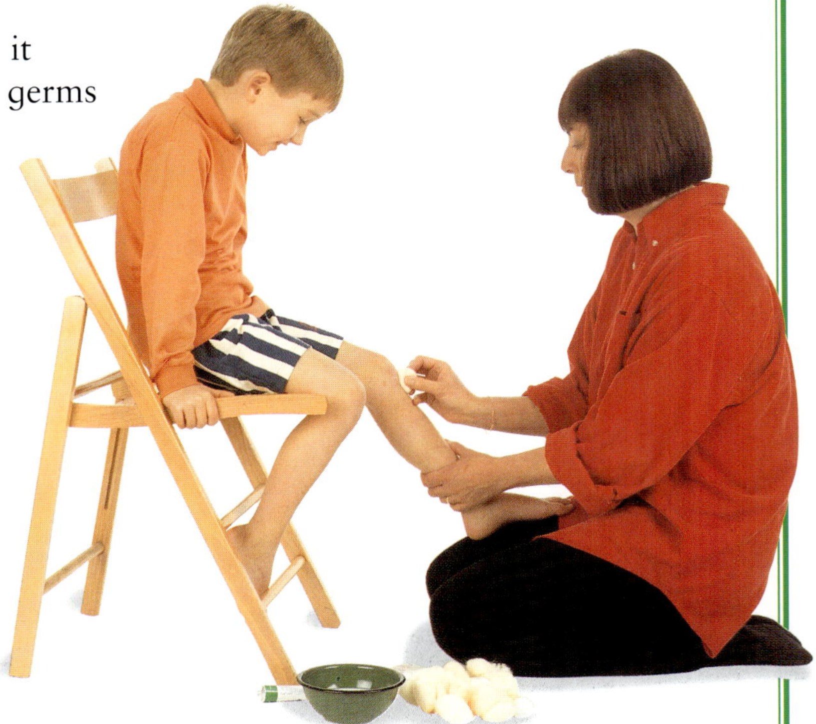

▽ Your body needs sleep to give your brain and muscles time to rest. When you are asleep, your body also has time to grow.

▷ Dentists look after teeth. If they find a hole, they make a filling. Don't eat too many sweets and brush your teeth every day to keep them clean.

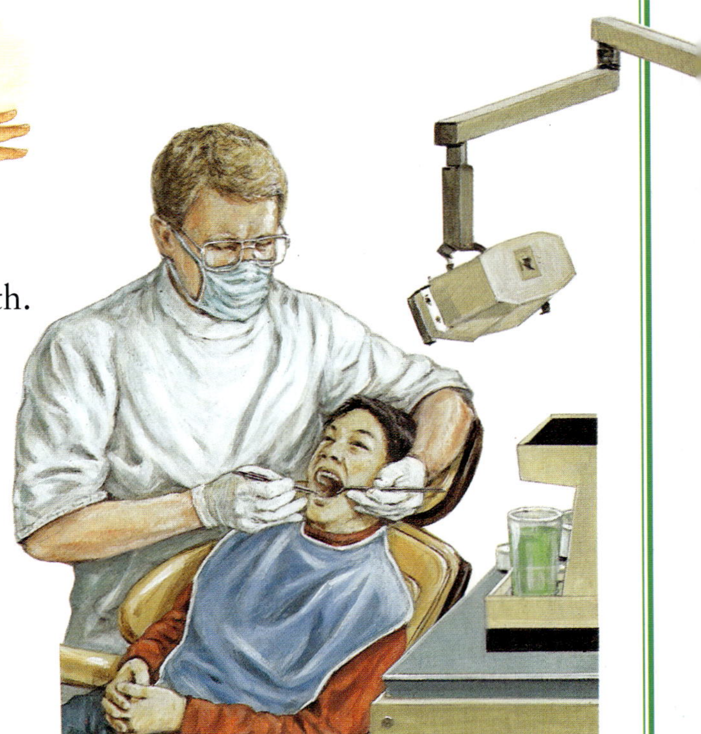

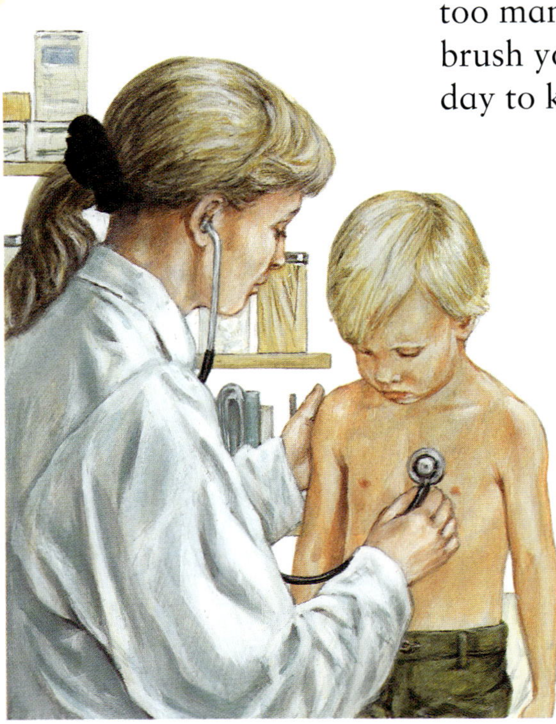

◁ Doctors look after you when you are ill. They may listen to your heart or look down your throat. If you need any medicine, they will give you this to help you get better.

Find out more

Conservation
Food
Human body
Sports
Water

History

History is the study of what happened in the past. Historians read old books, papers and manuscripts to discover the facts. They look for clues in paintings, old buildings, maps and photographs. Archaeologists study the things people made and used. They try to find ruined buildings and buried objects, such as tools, weapons and pots. These help to show how people lived long ago.

△ Older people can tell you about events and daily life when they were young. Their childhood was probably very different from yours.

◁ Archaeologists often dig in the ground or search underwater to find clues about houses, tombs, bones and many everyday objects.

△ Museums display objects from all over the world for people to come and see. Museums help all of us to learn more about the past.

▷ Reading books on history is a good way to find out about the past. Television and radio have history programmes too.

Ancient Egypt

Some Egyptian pharaohs were buried in pyramids. Their bodies were rowed down the Nile River and sealed inside a tomb filled with food, weapons and furniture.

△ People visit ancient sites like the pyramids to find out more about history. Paintings on the walls inside tell us how the Egyptians once lived.

Ancient Greece

The Greeks performed plays in open-air theatres. They had a circular floor for dancing with a stage behind. All the parts were played by men who wore masks.

△ The ruins of many Greek theatres are still standing. These tell us how the theatres looked.

Ancient China
The Great Wall of China is the longest wall ever built. It was built to keep out enemy tribes. The wall had towers for look-out posts.

▷ Some of the Great Wall of China still stands today. People like to walk along its top.

Ancient Americas
The Aztecs ruled a mighty empire in what is now Mexico. They were fierce warriors. They built pyramids with temples on top to make offerings to their gods.

△ Aztec men wore brooches like this one made of gold and turquoise to fasten their cloaks.

Second World War Many cities, like Cologne in Germany, were bombed in the Second World War. The war lasted for five years and many millions of people died.

▷ After the war, the buildings in Cologne were quickly rebuilt. This picture shows how it looks today.

◁ No one knows who carved these enormous stone heads on Easter Island in the Pacific Ocean. We are still learning about the past but some things may always stay a mystery.

Find out more

Art and artists
Books
Castles
Kings

Human body

Nobody in the world is exactly the same as you. You may be a girl or you may be a boy. Your skin could be light or it could be dark. Some people are tall and some are short, some are fat and some are thin. Although you look different from everybody else, your body is made up of the same parts as theirs. These parts all have important jobs to do to keep you alive and well.

△ The shape of our eyes, ears, noses and mouths, as well as the colour of our hair and skin, make us look different from each other.

The five senses
You can hear, see, smell, taste and feel things. These are called your five senses. Messages go from your ears, eyes, nose, mouth and skin to your brain. These tell you what the world is like and what is happening to your body.

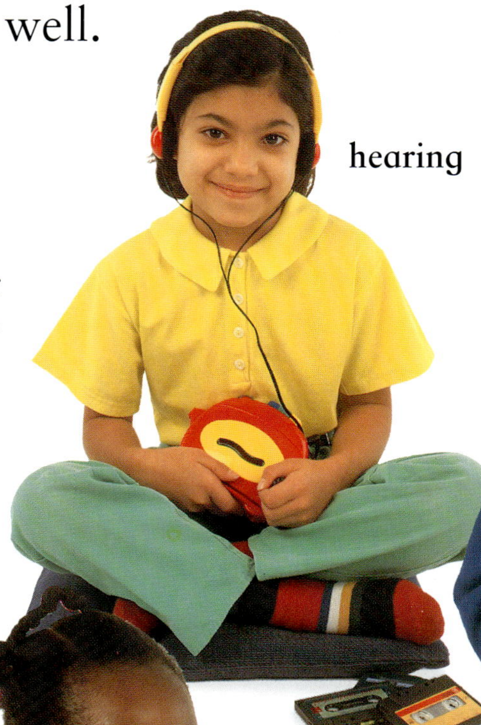

hearing

taste

sight

touch

smell

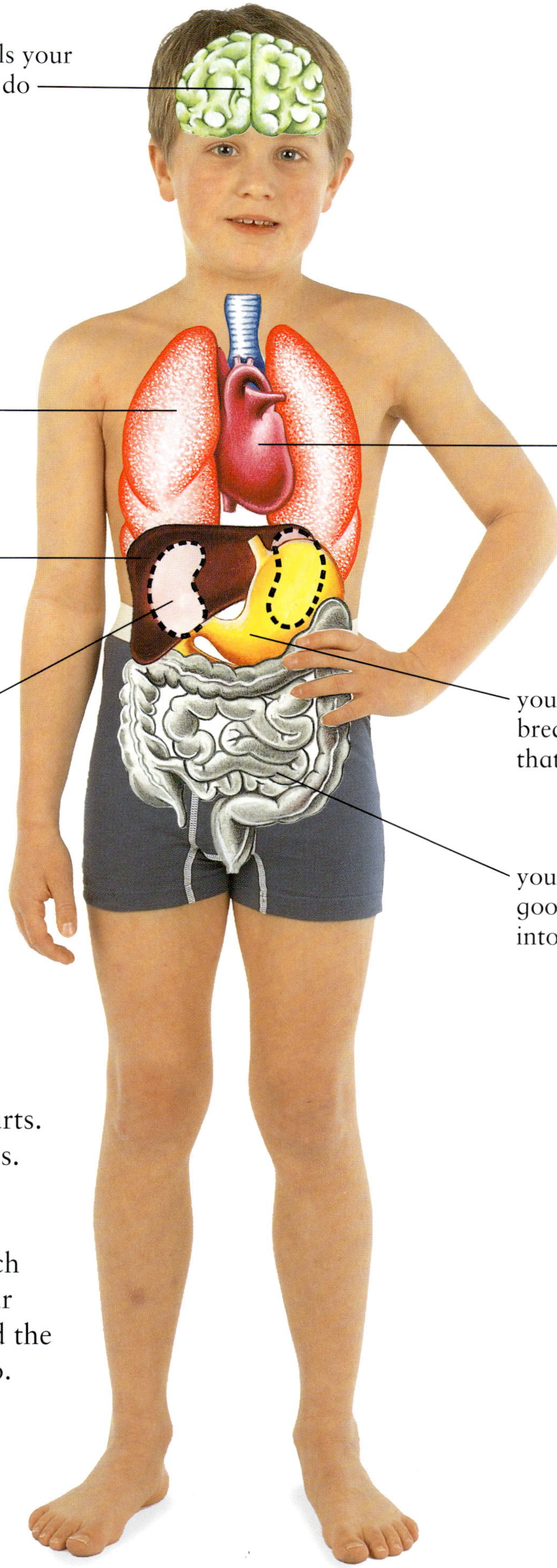

Inside your body

Inside your body there are many important working parts. These parts are called organs. Your brain, heart, lungs, stomach, liver, kidneys and intestines are all organs. Each organ has a special job. Your brain tells all the organs and the rest of your body what to do.

Skeleton

You have over 200 bones in your body. They are joined together to make your skeleton. Bones are hard and strong. They support your body and get bigger as you grow.

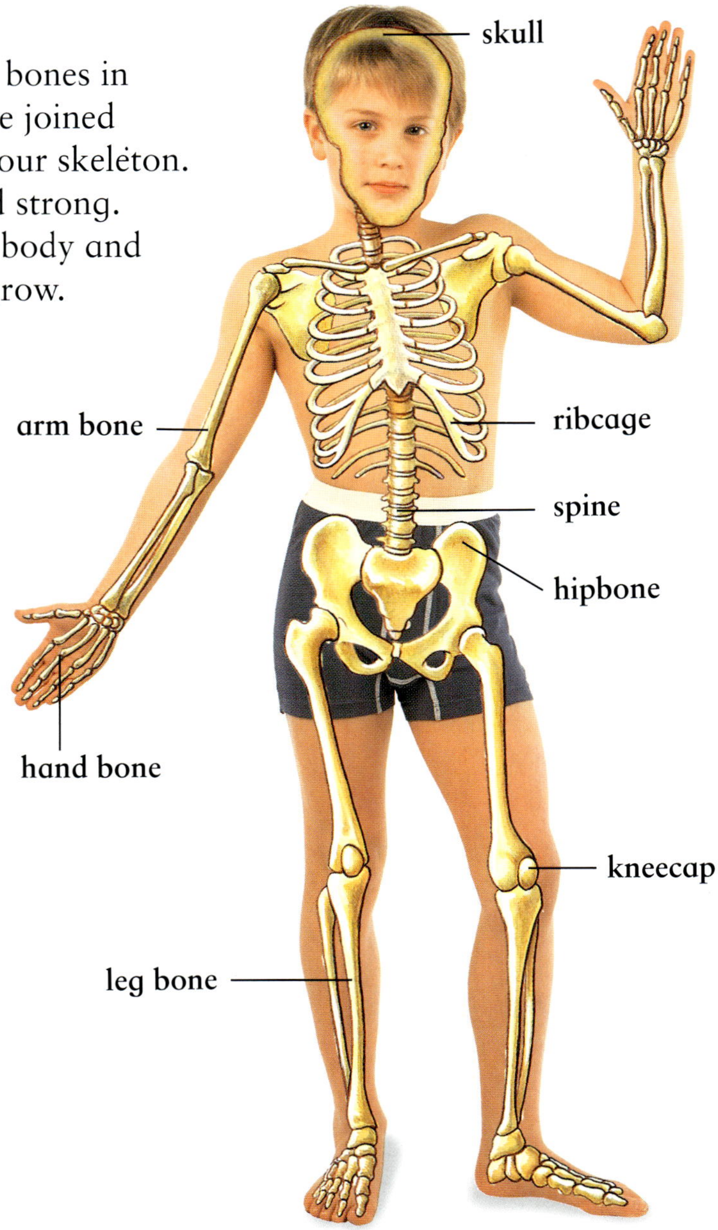

Muscles

All over your body you have muscles. These pull on your bones and make your body move. Muscles are joined to your bones by tough strips, called tendons. Muscles grow bigger and stronger with exercise.

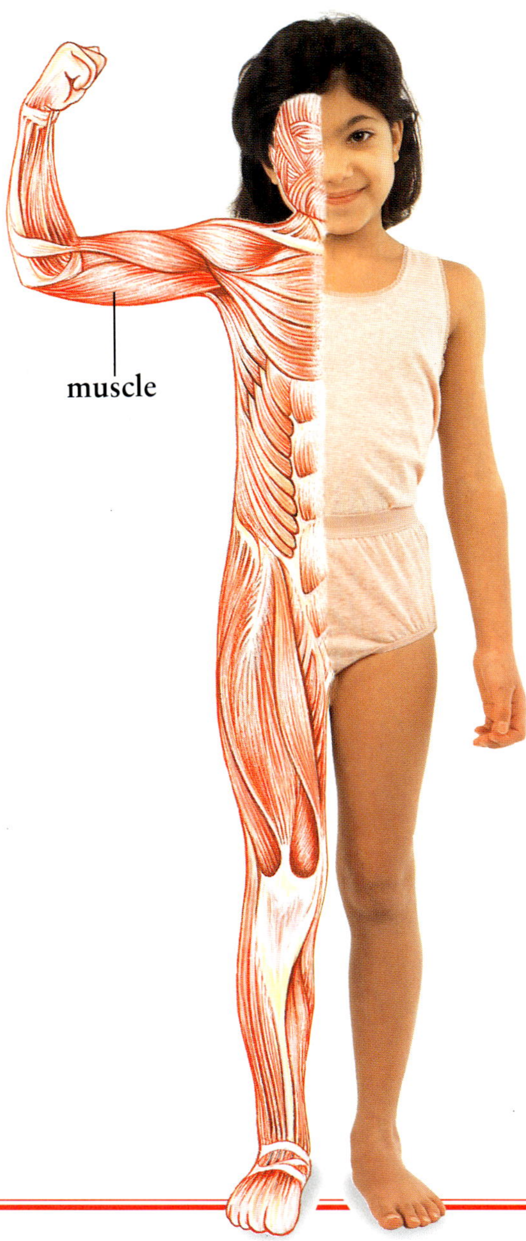

Breathing in

When you breathe in, air rushes into your lungs. Oxygen in the air mixes with the blood in your lungs. Your blood takes the oxygen to all parts of your body.

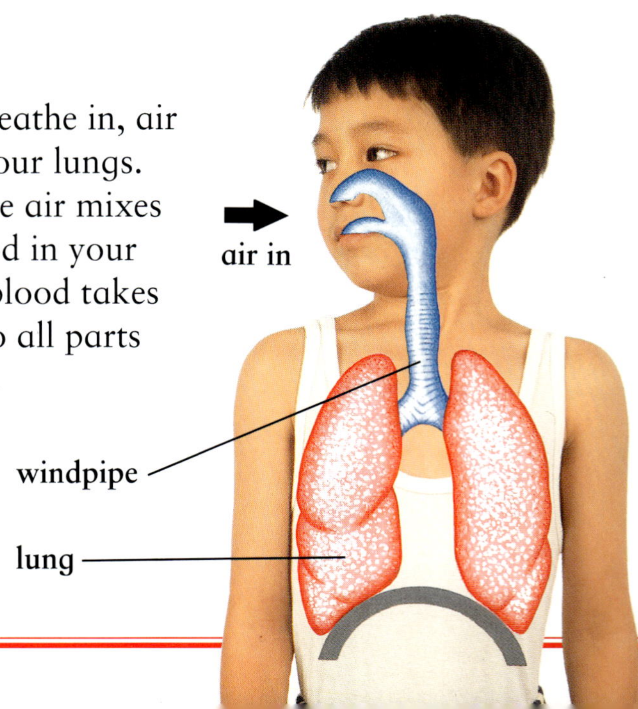

Circulation

Your heart is a big muscle. As it beats, it pumps blood around your body. Blood carries the food and oxygen your body needs to every part of the body. Blood flows through your body in tubes called veins and arteries.

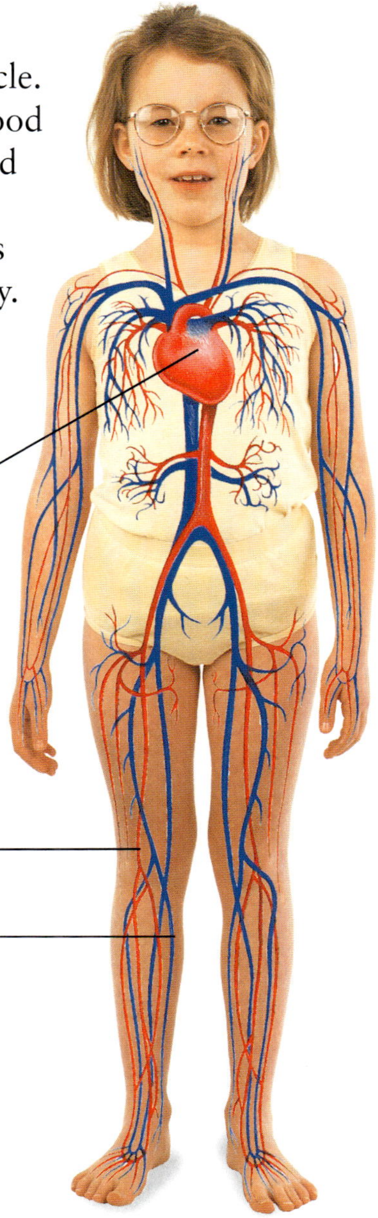

Skin

Tough, stretchy skin covers your whole body. It protects all the parts inside and keeps out dirt and germs. The skin also tells you what things feel like – hot, cold, rough, smooth or sharp.

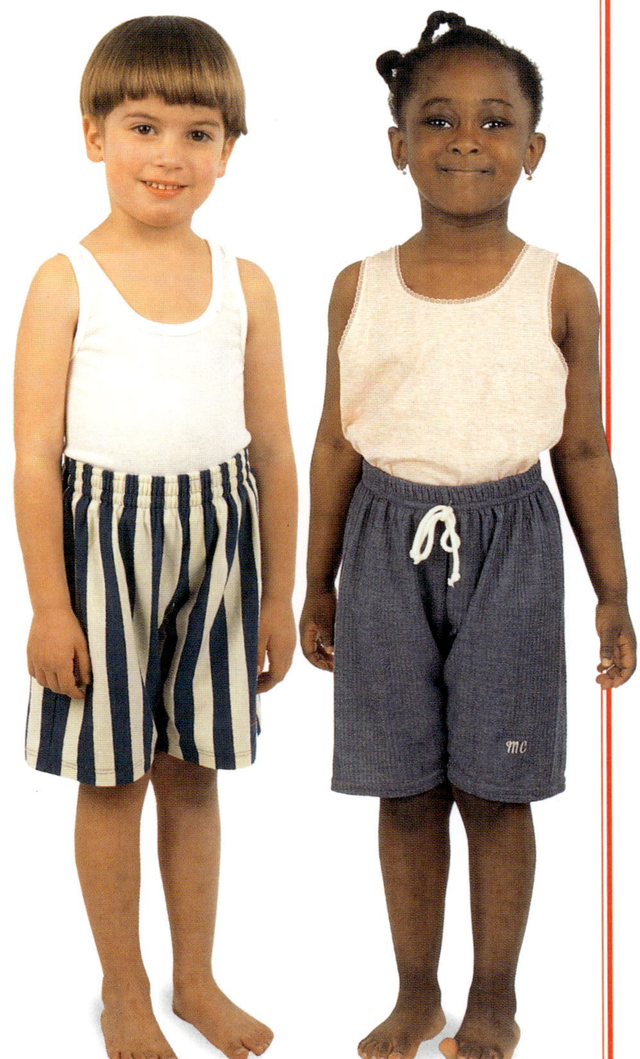

Breathing out

When you breathe out, the lungs empty and used air is pushed out.

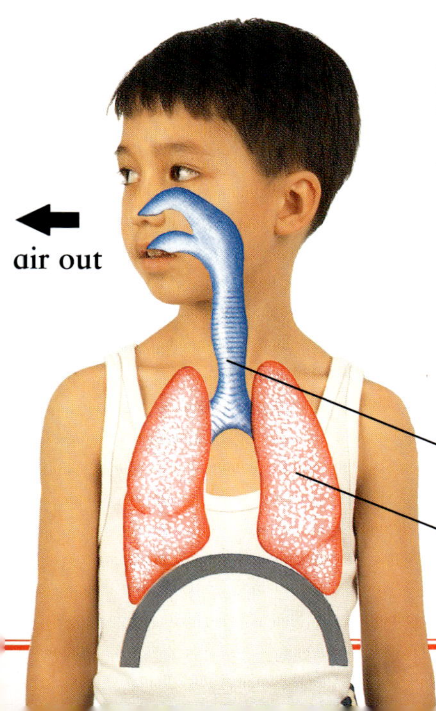

Find out more

Babies
Energy
Food
Health
Mammals
X-rays

Insects

Insects are animals with six legs. Most insects are tiny and have wings. Even the largest insect, the goliath beetle, is only ten centimetres long. Many insects are brightly coloured and some look like leaves or twigs to help them hide from their enemies.

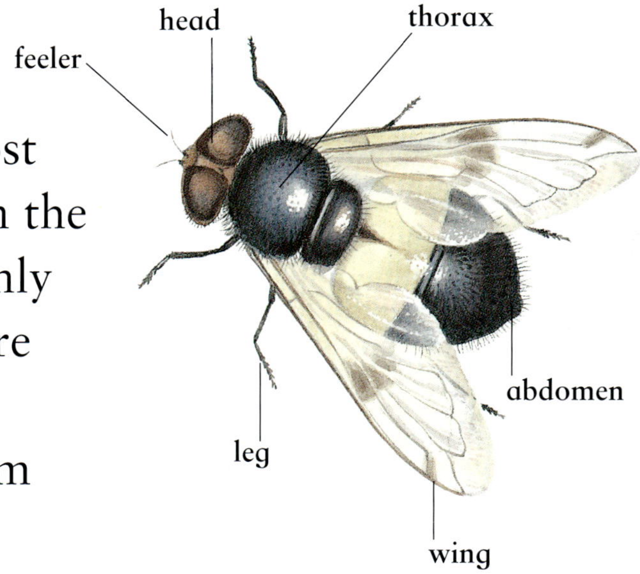

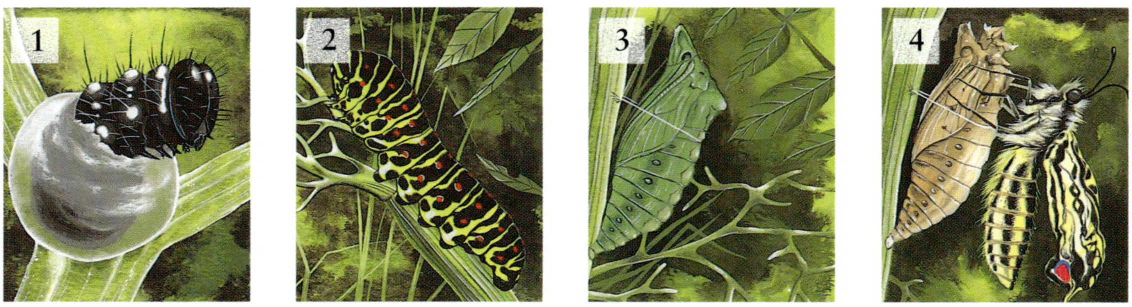

adult swallowtail butterfly

△ **1** A female butterfly lays eggs on a plant that her young will eat. Each egg hatches into a caterpillar. **2** A caterpillar eats greedily and grows quickly.

△ **3** The caterpillar turns into a chrysalis. **4** The adult butterfly bursts out of the chrysalis.

potter wasp

◁ A female potter wasp makes a clay pot for each of her eggs. She puts live caterpillars in each pot, so the baby wasp has food when it hatches.

△ The dragonfly is the fastest insect. It flies above ponds and streams hunting for other insects to eat.

bumble-bee

◁ Bees collect nectar and pollen from flowers. They take this to their nests to feed their grubs.

cockroach

▷ Cockroaches are unpleasant insects. They spoil our food and they often carry germs.

Fact Box

- An insect's body has three parts – the head, thorax and abdomen.
- Feelers are used to smell and feel.
- Some insects can taste with their feet.
- Most insects are less than six millimetres long.
- Ants live in big groups called colonies.

leaf-cutter ants

△ Leaf-cutter ants can lift leaves that are larger than themselves. They carry the leaves back to their nests.

goliath beetle

◁ This is the actual size of an adult goliath beetle. It can weigh as much as a mouse.

mosquito

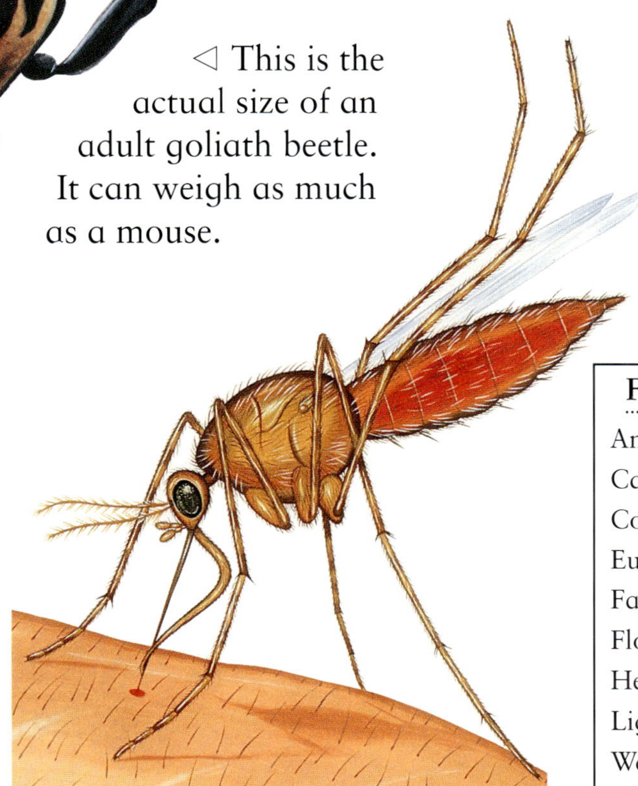

▷ A female mosquito sucks human and animal blood. It uses its sharp mouthparts to pierce the skin and suck up the blood through a tube.

Find out more

Animals
Camouflage
Colour
Europe
Farming
Flowers
Health
Light
Water

Inventions

Inventions are new ways of doing things. Some have made life more comfortable or have improved our health. Some have helped us to travel further and faster. Some have changed how we talk to one another. But not all inventions have been for the good. Guns and bombs have changed the way wars are fought.

△ Long ago, people discovered it was easier to roll heavy things. Then they invented the wheel.

wheel

fridge

△ A fridge keeps food and drink cool. Cool food stays fresher for longer. Before fridges were invented, people kept food cool with large blocks of ice.

▽ Plastic is made from chemicals in factories. It is a useful invention because it is easy to shape and it is tough. Lots of things are plastic.

▷ Television brings pictures and sounds from all over the world into our homes. We watch the TV to learn and to relax.

television

▽ An incubator is a warm, closed cot. It protects sick babies and ones that are born too early. They stay there until they are strong and well.

incubator

▷ This is a very old telescope. It was built by Galileo, a famous astronomer. He used it to look at the Moon and the planets.

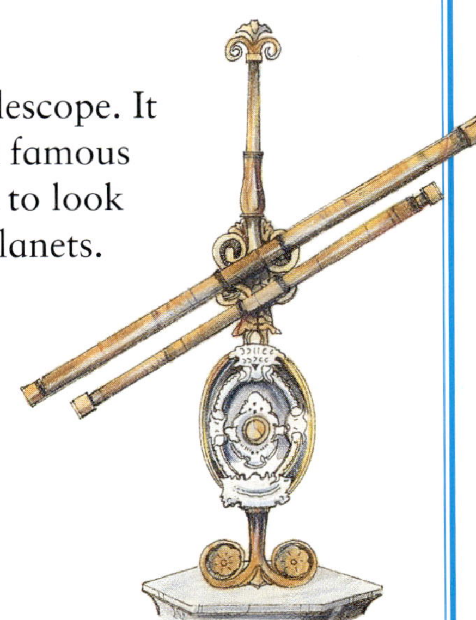

telescope

▽ Using a camera to take photographs is an easy way to keep a record of people, places and events you have seen.

▽ The invention of the telephone makes it possible for you to talk to someone else almost anywhere in the world.

camera

telephone

Find out more

Bikes
Books
Cars
Computers
Flying machines
Trains
Space exploration

Jobs

People do all sorts of jobs. They may farm or fish. They may make things in a factory or sell things in a shop. They may build homes, drive trucks or look after ill people. People work to earn money. They may start jobs when they leave school or college and stop work when they get old.

△ Teachers work in schools. They help children to learn the things they need to know.

△ Farming is an important job all over the world. This man is cutting sugar cane.

△ Many people work in offices. They use computers and telephones to help them.

△ Supermarkets provide jobs. This man is arranging food on the shelves.

▷ These people are making a film. Each has a different job, such as acting, directing, recording the sound and filming.

Find out more
Books
Computers
Farming
Fishing

Kings

A king is a man who rules a country or people. Usually the king's son becomes the next king. Some kings are called chiefs or emperors. In the past, kings made laws and led their people into battle. Today, kings have less power. Most countries do not have kings at all.

△ This gold mask shows the face of Tutankhamun, a young king of Ancient Egypt. The Egyptians called their kings pharaohs.

△ This is the king of Tonga and his family at a wedding. His family has ruled Tonga for 200 years.

▽ The British Crown Jewels are only worn on special occasions. Kings once wore crowns as a sign of power.

◁ Kings often lived in large houses, called palaces, or castles. This palace was the home of the emperors of China.

Find out more
Castles
History

Light

Almost all our light comes from the Sun. Light is a type of energy. It travels from the Sun, through Space at very high speed. Light is the fastest thing in the Universe.

Light is made by hot or burning things. Flames, fireworks and light bulbs all give off light. Some animals can make their own light.

△ During the day, we see by sunlight. At night, we use electric lights to see.

▷ Early people burned animal oil in stone lamps to make light. Later candles were used. Two hundred years ago people used oil lamps. Today we use electric lights.

stone lamp

wax candle

oil lamp

electric light bulb

▽ A glow-worm is a type of beetle that makes its own pale green light. The female uses the light to attract a mate in the dark.

glow-worm

transparent

△ Glass is transparent. It lets light pass through. You can see through glass clearly.

translucent

△ Plastic is translucent. It lets some light through. You cannot see through clearly.

opaque

△ Thick paper is opaque. It stops all light. You cannot see through opaque things at all.

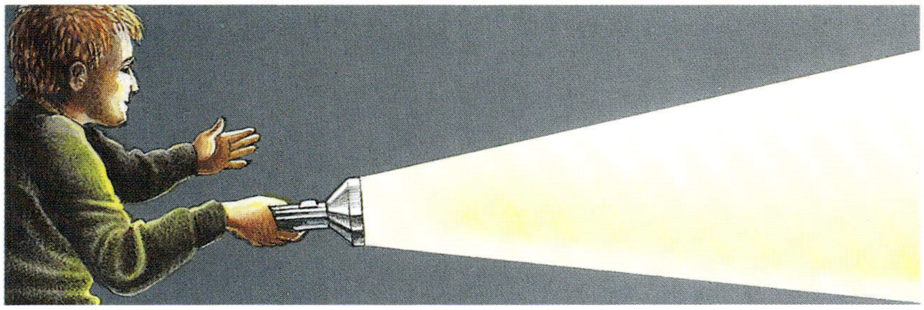

◁ Light always travels in straight lines. Light can spread out, but it cannot bend around things.

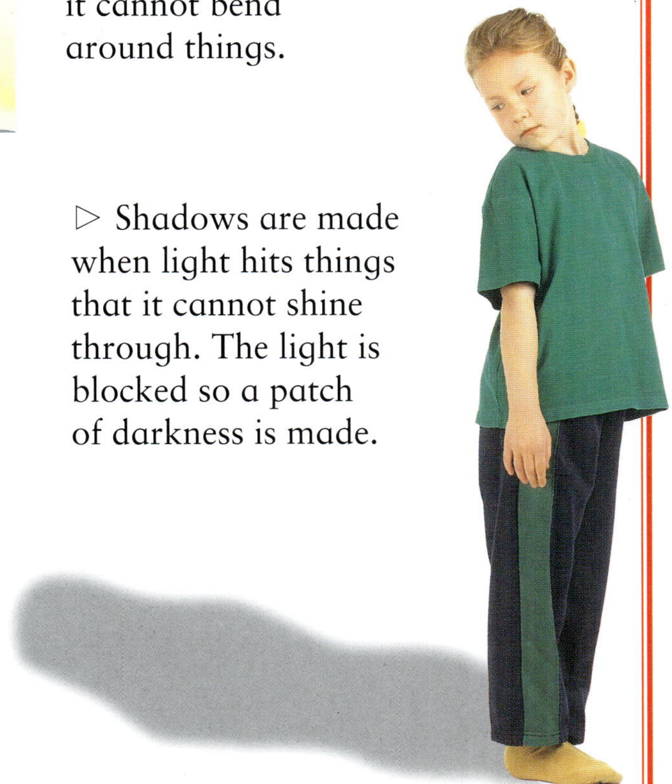

▷ Shadows are made when light hits things that it cannot shine through. The light is blocked so a patch of darkness is made.

△ You can see yourself in water because light bounces off its surface into your eyes. This is a reflection.

△ A rainbow shows us the colours in sunlight. When the Sun shines through rain, the light is split up into all its different colours.

◁ A tomato looks red to you because it soaks up all the colours in sunlight, except red. The red bounces off it, into your eyes.

Find out more

Antarctica and Arctic
Colour
Earth
Electricity
Plants
Sun

Machines

Machines are used to help people do things. Some machines are very complicated, with lots of moving parts. Others are very simple. We use simple machines every day. There are six types of simple machine: the lever, the wheel and axle, the slope, the wedge, the pulley and the screw. All these machines make it easier to move things.

△ Levers make it easier to lift things. This boy gently pushes down on the long handle to lift the stiff lid off the jar.

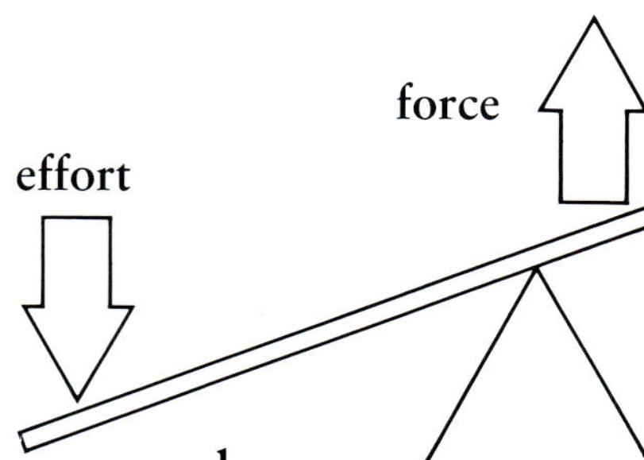

▽ The axle turns the wheels to move this tricycle along. It is much easier to roll a heavy object on wheels than it is to drag it along the ground.

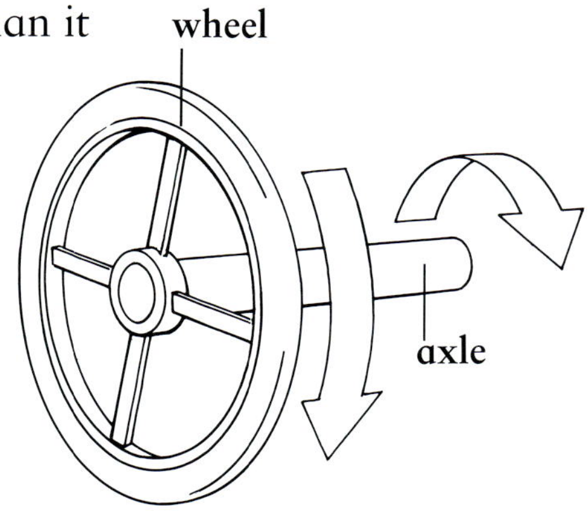

▽ A slope makes it easier for this man to move the heavy wheel-barrow upwards. It is easier to push it along instead of lifting it up.

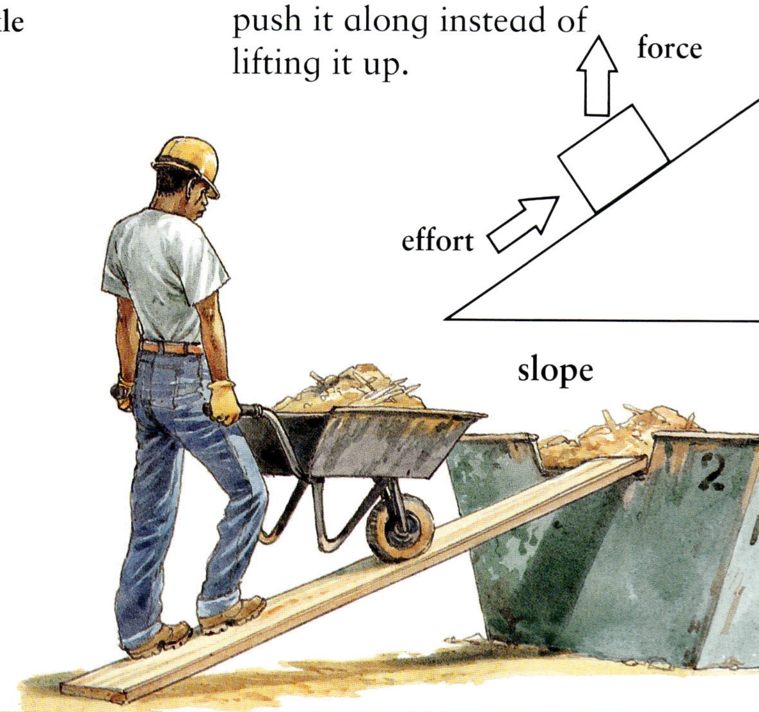

▽ This man is splitting logs with an axe. The axe blade is a wedge. Wedges force things apart. When the man brings down the axe, the blade forces the log to split sideways.

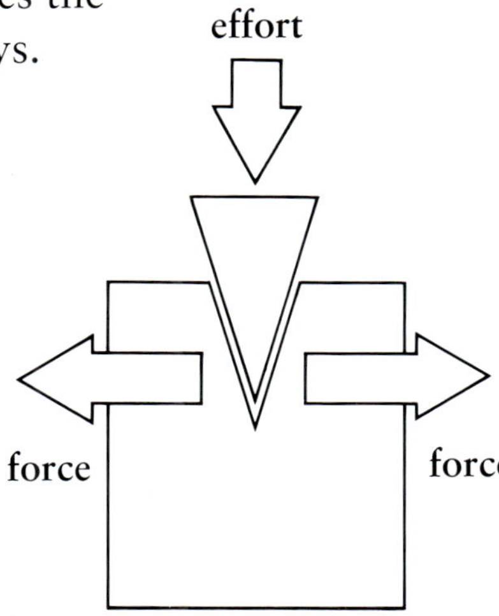

wedge

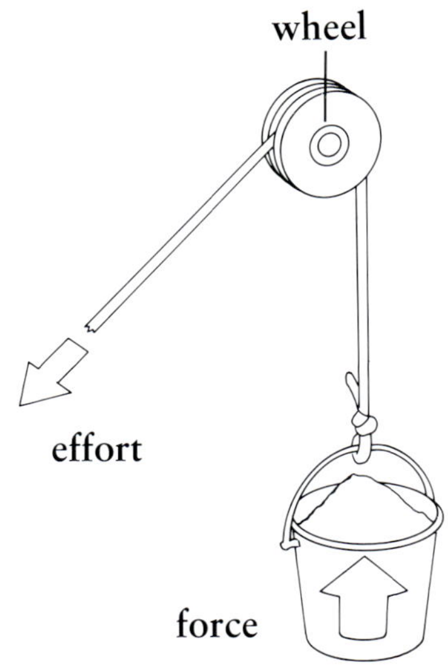

pulley

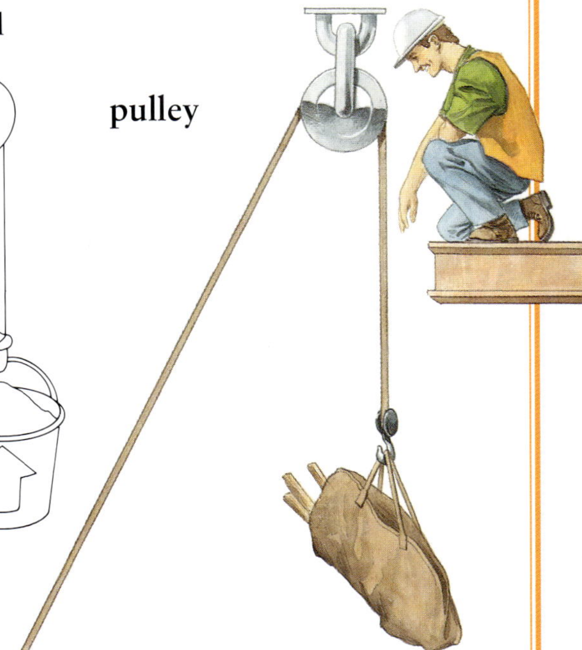

△ A pulley has a wheel with a rope fitted over it. The man pulls down on the rope to lift the heavy load at the other end.

▷ Screws are used to fasten things together. When the girl turns the screw and nut, they squeeze the two pieces of wood tightly together. Screws are also used to lift things.

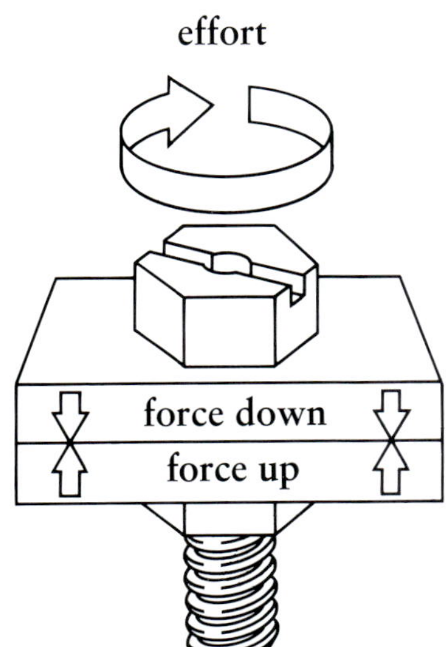

screw

Complicated machines
Several simple machines can be put together to make much more complicated machines.

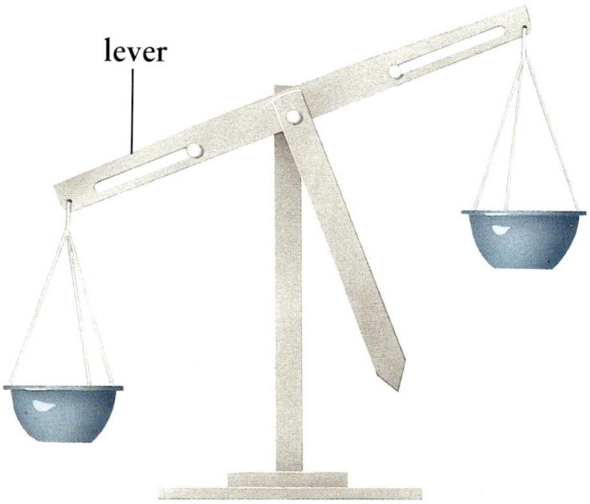

△ This type of weighing scale is a lever. When a load is put in one bowl, it falls. The other bowl rises. If each bowl has an equal load, the scales balance.

△ Clocks have cogs inside them. Cogs are wheels with teeth that fit between one another. The cogs in a clock turn the hands at different speeds.

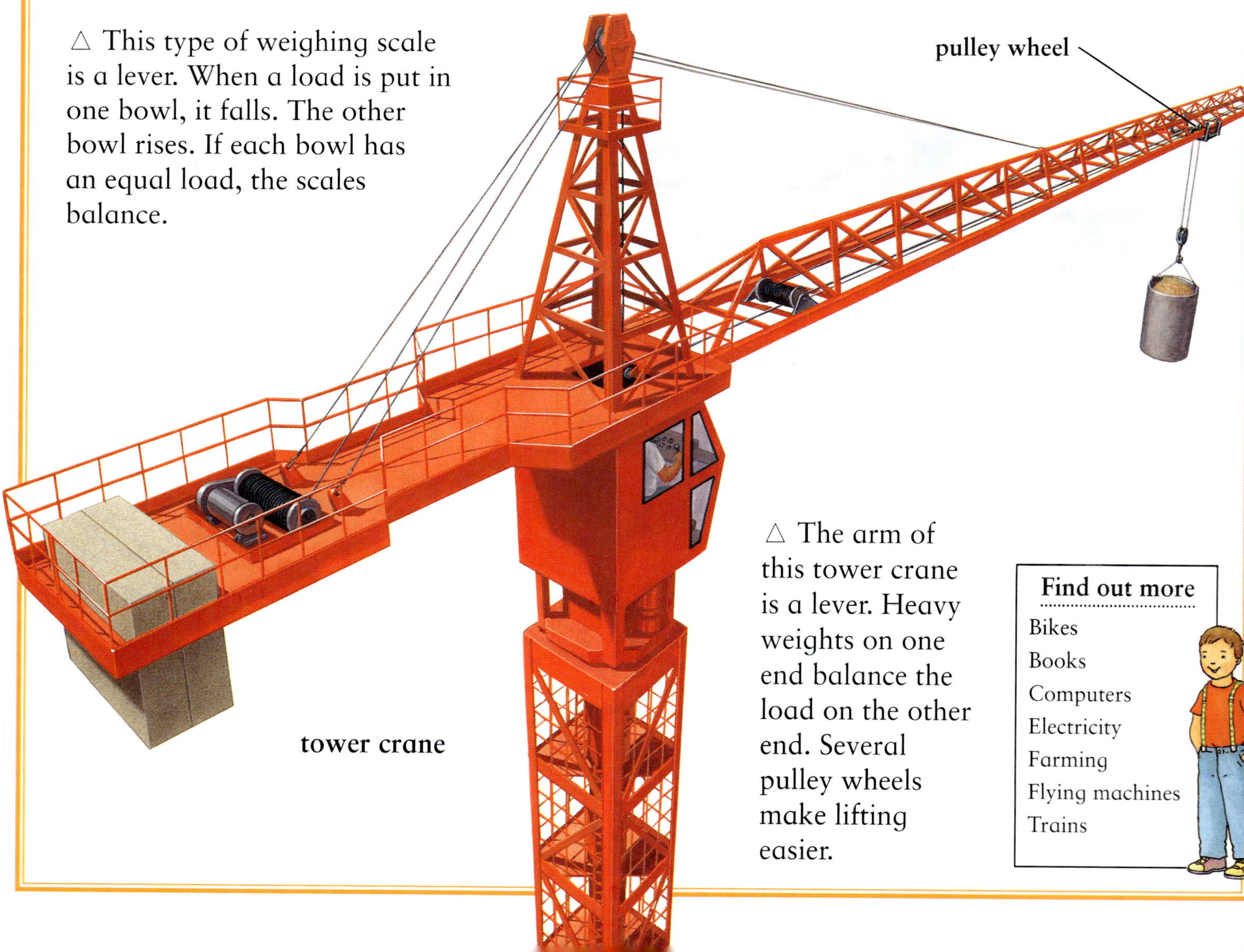

△ The arm of this tower crane is a lever. Heavy weights on one end balance the load on the other end. Several pulley wheels make lifting easier.

Find out more
Bikes
Books
Computers
Electricity
Farming
Flying machines
Trains

Magnets

Magnets attract, or pull, certain things towards them. Objects made of some metals, such as iron and steel, are attracted to a magnet. Materials that are attracted to a magnet are called magnetic. Most materials, such as wood, cloth, paper, glass, plastic and some other metals are not magnetic.

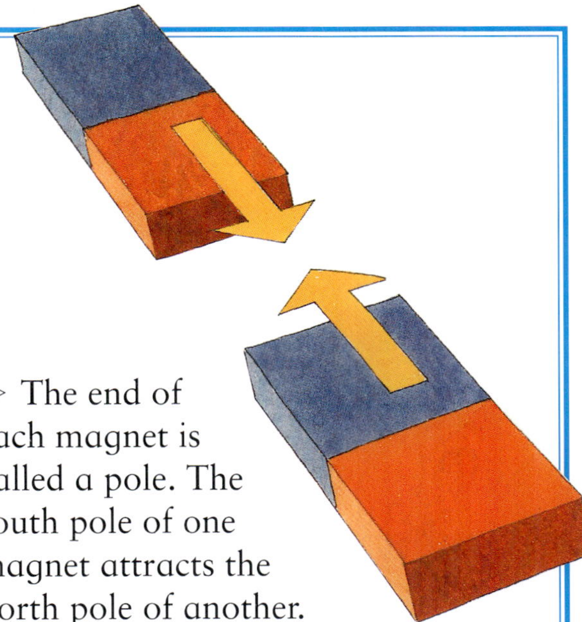

▷ The end of each magnet is called a pole. The south pole of one magnet attracts the north pole of another.

▷ You can find out for yourself which things are magnetic. Collect a pile of objects and see how many you can pick up with a magnet. Can you spot the magnetic things in this picture?

◁ Giant magnets like this one are used to pick up and move huge pieces of metal, such as old cars.

Find out more

Metals

Mammals

Mammals are animals whose young are fed with their mother's milk. Most mammals give birth to live young.

The biggest mammal is the blue whale, which can be as long as six elephants. One of the smallest is a kind of bat that is about the size of a bumble bee.

rabbit

△ A rabbit gives birth to lots of babies at the same time. A mother rabbit cares for her young until they can look after themselves.

humans

◁ Humans are mammals too. When we are babies we are fed with our mother's milk.

kangaroo

▷ A kangaroo is a marsupial, a mammal that carries its young in a pouch. A baby kangaroo is called a joey.

lion

cubs

▷ Lions live in family groups called prides. They eat meat and are fierce hunters. A lioness cares for her cubs and teaches them how to hunt.

mole

▽ A mole is a burrowing mammal. It has strong front legs and big claws for digging holes called burrows.

dolphins

◁ Dolphins are mammals that live in the sea. They have to come to the surface to breathe.

bat

△ Bats are the only mammals that can fly. A bat has a furry body and its wings are soft, smooth skin.

chimpanzees

△ Chimpanzees live in family groups. They often comb each other's hair with their fingers and pick off dirt and ticks.

Fact box

- Most mammals have either hair or fur.
- Mammals are warm-blooded. This means that the temperature of their bodies stays the same in both hot and cold weather.
- A mammal is a vertebrate, which means that it has a backbone.
- Mammals have larger brains than other animals.

▽ The duck-billed platypus is an unusual mammal because it lays eggs.

duck-billed platypus

Etruscan shrew

△ The tiny Etruscan shrew weighs no more than a sugar lump.

lioness

Find out more

Animals
Australia and the Pacific Islands
Babies
Caves
Grasslands
Human body
Prehistoric life
Soil

Maps

A map is a carefully drawn picture that shows you what a place looks like from above. Maps show things like roads and rivers. They can help you to find your way from one place to another. Maps are drawn to show a large area of land much smaller than it really is. A book of maps is called an atlas.

▽ Make a map of the area around your home. Draw in the streets and add any important landmarks, such as your school, shops or a park.

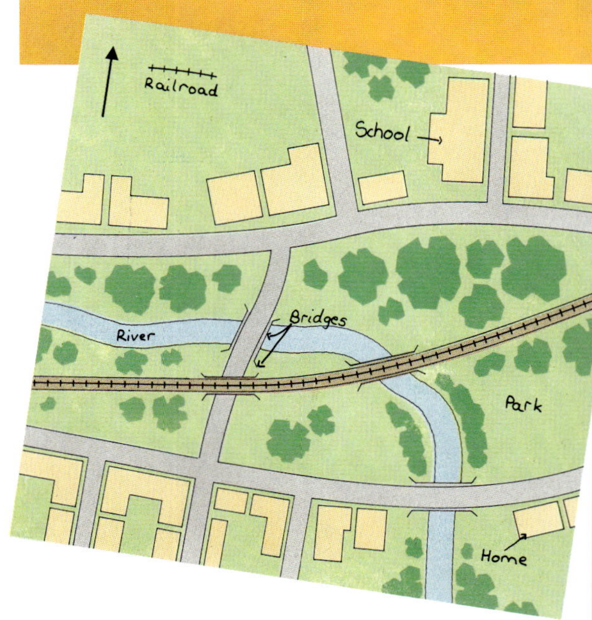

△ From the air, the area around the Eiffel Tower in Paris looks like this.

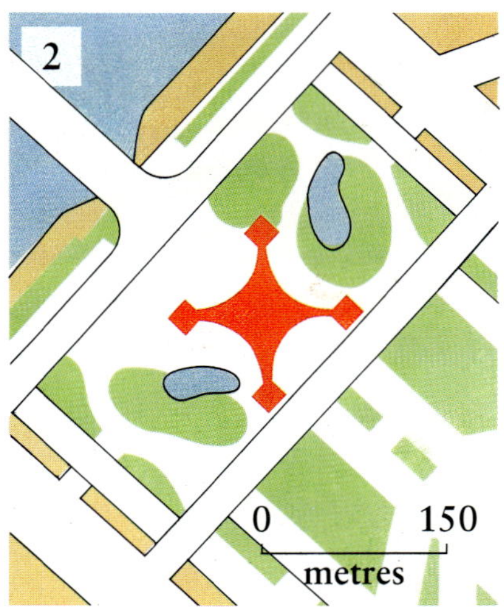

△ This map shows the small area around the Eiffel Tower in detail.

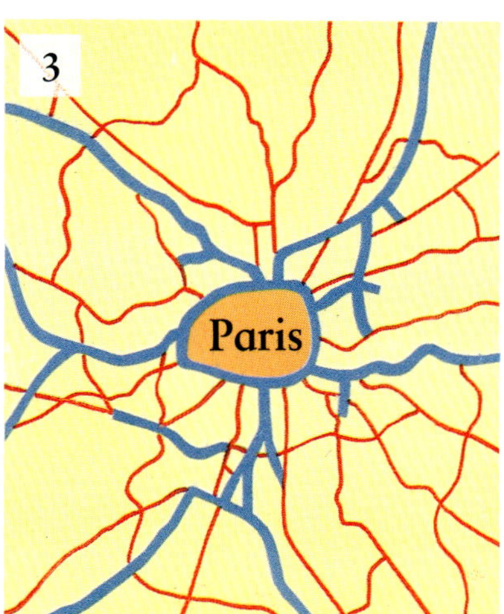

◁ The road map on the left shows a much larger area. You can see Paris, but you can't see the Tower.

◁ This map is of the whole of France. You can see Paris, but you can't see all the roads around the city.

Find out more
World

Measuring

If you want to find out how heavy or tall things are, you can measure them exactly using different instruments. In the past, people used their hands, arms or feet instead of centimetres for measuring. This was a problem, because no one was the same size. Now, people use the same measurements.

▽ Long ago, the Egyptians used hand spans, like this, to measure how long or wide things were. Today we use rulers or tape measures.

◁ Scales are used to find out how heavy things are. This is called weight. Weight is measured in grams and kilograms.

▷ You use a ruler or tape measure to find out how long or high something is. Length and height are measured in metres and centimetres.

▷ A measuring jug is used to find out how much liquid is needed. Liquids are measured in litres.

Find out more

Antarctica and Arctic
Time
Weather

Metals

Metals are quite often hard, shiny materials. They can be bent or hammered into different shapes. Iron, copper and aluminium are three kinds of metal. Most metals come from ores, which are a mixture of metal and rock. The ore is dug out of the ground. Different metals can be mixed to make tough, new metals, called alloys.

△ Aluminium is used to make foil, cans and pipes, copper is used for saucepans, steel for scissors and paperclips, and gold and silver are used to make jewellery.

△ Iron ore is heated in a furnace. When it gets very hot, the iron melts. The iron is then poured off, leaving the unwanted rock behind. The iron is then used to make steel.

▽ Iron turns rusty if it is left in damp air. Rusty metal is weak and crumbles away. Often metal things are specially treated to stop them rusting.

Find out more
Buildings
Magnets
Money

Money

Money is used to pay for the things we want to buy. Coins and paper notes are money. Each coin and note is worth a different amount. People use notes for large amounts. Notes are printed with complicated patterns that are hard to fake, or copy.

△ Before money existed, people swapped the things they needed. This is called barter. The man on the left is bartering his cattle for armour.

▷ You can save your coins in a money box. Large amounts of money are kept in a bank.

◁ Each country has its own type of money. Great Britain uses pounds, America uses dollars and France uses the euro.

Find out more
Jobs
Metal

Moon

The Moon is our nearest neighbour in Space. It is a large ball of dusty rock with no air, water, wind or weather. No animals or plants can live there. During the day it is boiling hot, but at night it is very cold. The Moon looks bright in the sky because it reflects light from the Sun.

△ The Moon is covered with dents called craters. These were made when meteoroids crashed into the Moon. Meteoroids are large lumps of rock and metal.

▽ The Moon moves around the Earth once every month. Its path is called an orbit.

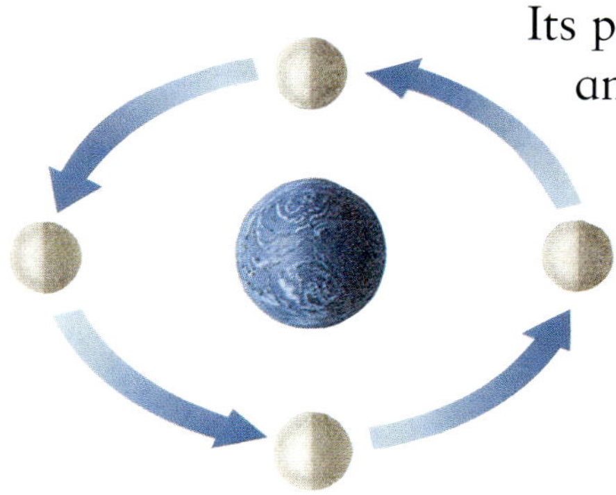

Full Moon

△ There is a Full Moon once a month. As the Sun lights up different parts of the Moon, its shape seems to change.

▽ On 20th July 1969, two American astronauts were the first people to set foot on the Moon. They were called Neil Armstrong and Buzz Aldrin.

Find out more
Planets
Space exploration

Mountains

A mountain is a piece of ground that is much higher than the land around it. The highest peaks are cold and windy. They are often covered with snow all year. Tough pine trees grow on the lower slopes. Above a certain height, it is too cold for trees to grow.

◁ Skiing is a fast way to get across snow. It is a popular mountain sport.

rocky mountain goat

△ Mountain goats have thick, woolly coats and are good climbers.

trumpet gentian

△ The cold winds mean that mountain plants can only grow in low clumps.

Find out more

Asia
Europe
Oceans and seas
South America
Volcano

Music

Most people love to play or listen to music. They may sing or play a musical instrument, like a piano or a guitar, by themselves or in a band or orchestra. People play music to celebrate special occasions, to entertain themselves or others, or just to relax. A person who makes music is called a musician. There are many different kinds of music.

△ You probably listen to music on tapes, CDs and records at home, or hear it on the radio and television.

△ An orchestra is a large group of musicians who play a variety of different instruments. Orchestras often play the music at concerts, operas or plays.

▷ At carnival time in the Caribbean islands, steel bands play in the streets or on the beach. The steel drums are made out of specially shaped, empty oil drums.

▷ This Japanese robot can play the keyboard much faster than a human can. It can read music or play a tune that is stored in its memory.

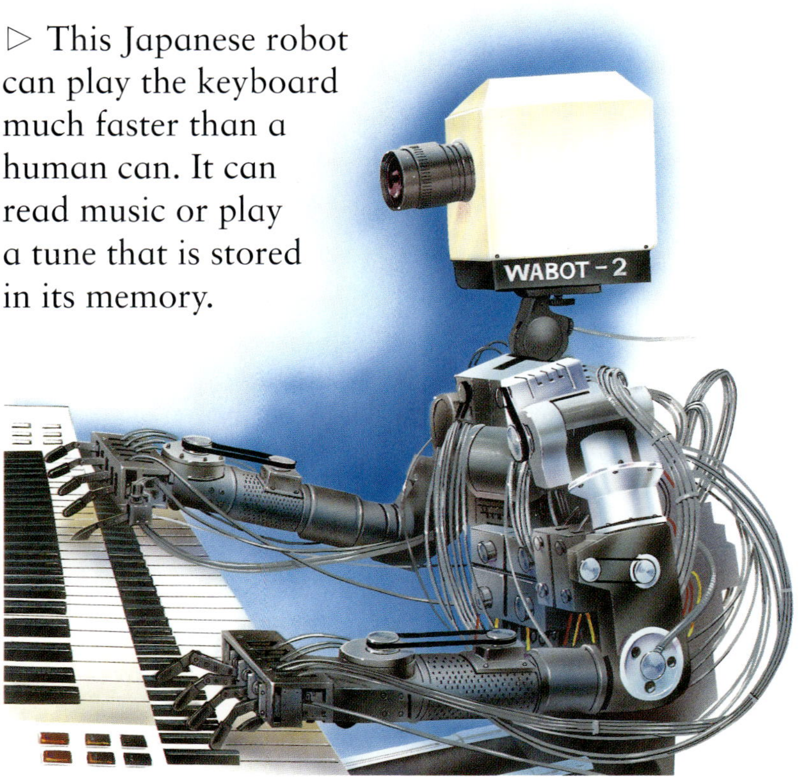

▽ You can play music too. You may know how to play the piano or the recorder. There are many other kinds of musical instruments. These children are making music with their instruments.

◁ One of the most famous musicians was Wolfgang Amadeus Mozart. It's hard to believe that he wrote his first piece of music when he was only five years old.

Find out more
Australia
Dance
Sound

North America

North America is the third largest continent. In the north it is cold and there are large forests and many lakes. In the south there are hot deserts and thick rainforests. The middle is a huge area of flat grassland, called the prairie. The magnificent Rocky Mountains run down one side. Many of its people live in busy, modern cities.

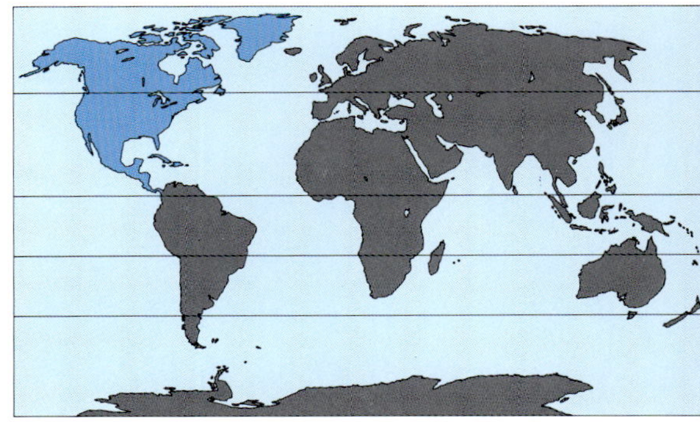

△ North America is shown in blue on this map. Most of it is covered by two very large countries, Canada and the United States of America.

◁ Many people visit Las Vegas in the USA. It was built in the middle of the desert. At night its buildings are lit up with their bright lights.

△ A teacher and her class at a school in the United States. People of many different nationalities have come to live and work in America.

◁ A stall owner getting ready for market day in Oaxaca, in Mexico. Mexican farmers were the first people to grow chillies, tomatoes, avocados, maize and many kinds of beans.

△ Thanksgiving Day is a national holiday in America. Families gather together to eat a traditional meal of roast turkey and pumpkin pie.

▽ The Grand Canyon in Arizona is one of the most famous sights in the United States. It was carved by a river flowing through the desert.

◁ Raccoons live in many parts of North America. They usually hunt at night for food.

raccoon

▷ The Niagara Falls lie on the border between Canada and the United States. Tourists take boats to see the base of the falls.

◁ The word pueblo is Spanish for village. Pueblo are Native American people who live in south-western USA.

Find out more

Buildings
Desert
Grasslands
History
Sports
World
Year

Oceans and seas

There are four huge areas of water called oceans – the Pacific, the Atlantic, the Indian and the Arctic. The Pacific is by far the biggest and deepest ocean. Seas are smaller areas of water. There is more water than land on the Earth's surface. You can sail right around the world without touching land.

△ Most waves are made by wind blowing across the water. Surfers ride on them before they crash on to the shore. Some waves are ten metres tall.

◁ There are strange animals in the deepest, darkest parts of the ocean. Some have large mouths and glowing lights to help them catch their prey.

▽ At the bottom of the ocean there are flat areas, trenches, hills and high mountains. Some islands are the tops of underwater volcanoes.

▷ There are billions of tiny plants and animals floating in the sea. They are called plankton. Many fish and other sea creatures feed on them.

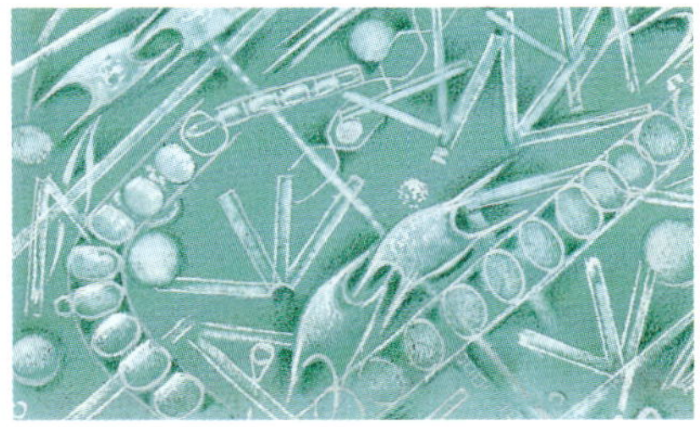

plankton

sperm whale

◁ Whales are the largest creatures in the ocean. This sperm whale can grow up to 20 metres long.

▽ An octopus has eight long arms. If an octopus loses an arm, it grows a new one.

blue ringed octopus

▷ For hundreds of years ships have sunk to the bottom of the sea. Divers sometimes find treasure in the remains of these ships.

▽ Divers use small submersibles to explore very deep water. They dive down to search for shipwrecks and to study ocean life.

submersible

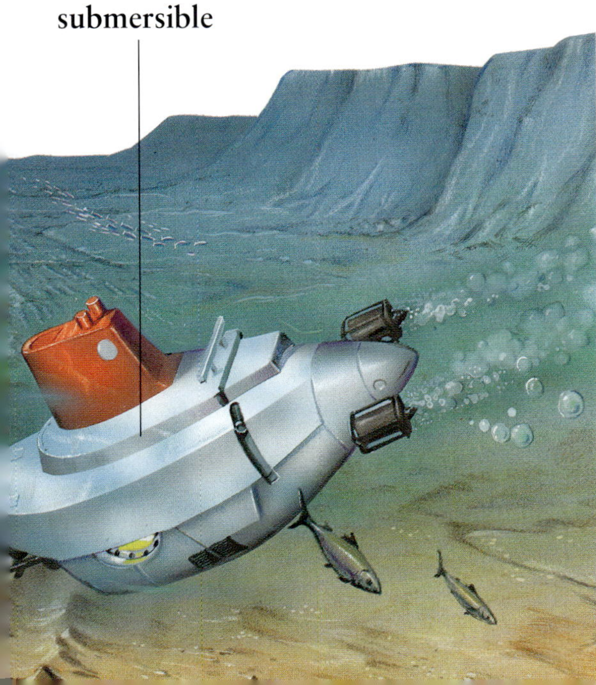

▽ Hot water bubbles up through chimney-like holes on the sea bed. Blind crabs, giant worms and other unusual creatures live near these rare hot spots.

worms

crabs

Find out more

Animals
Antarctica and Arctic
Art and artists
Australia and the Pacific Islands
Fish
Fishing
Mammals
Seashore
Ships and boats
Water
World

Planets

Planets are huge balls of rock, metal and gas that travel around a star. Earth is one of the nine planets that travel around our star, the Sun. The Sun, and all of the planets, moons and lumps of rock, dust and ice that whirl around it, make up the Solar System. Earth only has one moon travelling around it, but some planets have several.

△ The planets travel around the Sun in fixed paths, called orbits. Earth takes one year, or just over 365 days, to orbit the Sun.

Fact box

- Mercury is the closest planet to the Sun.
- Venus is the hottest planet. It is covered with thick clouds of poisonous gas.
- Earth is the only planet with air and water.
- Mars is a red, rocky planet. It is very dry and has dust storms.

Fact box

- Uranus orbits the Sun tipped on its side.
- Jupiter is the biggest planet. Its red spot is a giant whirlpool about the same size as Earth.
- Saturn has the brightest rings of all the planets. It has at least 18 moons orbiting it.

Fact box

- Saturn, Jupiter, Uranus and Neptune are giant planets and are all made of gas and liquid.
- Freezing winds rip across Neptune's blue surface.
- Pluto is the coldest, smallest planet. It is the farthest away from the Sun.

Find out more
Earth
Inventions
Moon
Space exploration
Sun
Universe

Plants

Plants grow all over the world. The biggest plants are trees and the smallest are so tiny that they can hardly be seen. Without plants, people and animals would not be able to live. They need plants for food. They also need to breathe the oxygen which comes from plants. Plants use the carbon dioxide that people and animals breathe out.

△ Most plants can make food from air, sunlight and water. They take in water through their roots.

▽ Edelweiss grows in snowy places. It has hairs on its stalks and leaves that trap heat to protect it from the cold.

△ A giant saguaro cactus can live for over 200 years. It survives in the hot, dry desert because it stores water in its thick stem.

◁ Some plants that grow in water have strong roots to anchor them in the soft mud. Others just float in the water.

▷ Some plants cannot make their own food. The dodder plant is a parasite, which means it attaches itself to another plant and steals its food.

▷ Plants like ivy can climb up buildings or tall trees. It clings tightly to rocks and walls with tiny roots.

▷ **1** A seed fills with water. It splits open and starts growing. **2** A root grows down into the soil. **3** A leafy shoot grows up out of the soil towards the Sun.

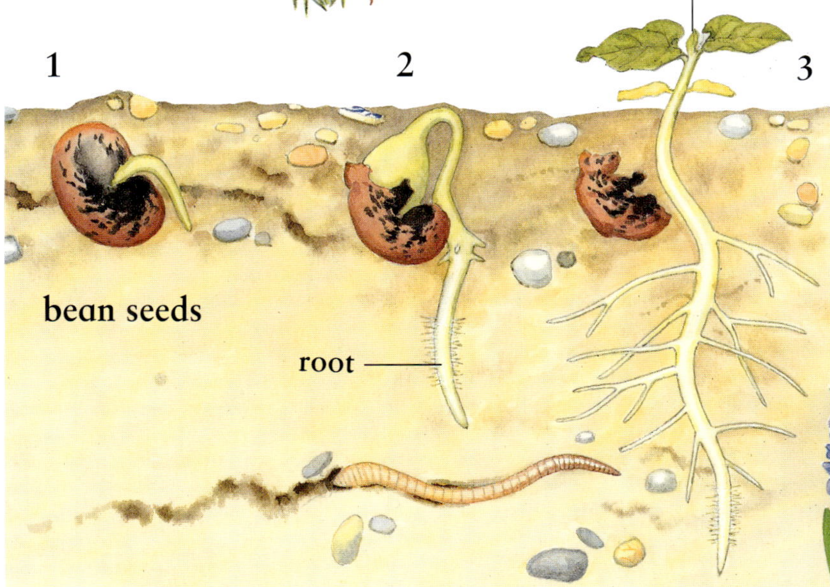

▷ Daffodils and hyacinths grow from bulbs. The bulbs store food all through the winter and grow into new plants in the spring.

fern

moss

△ Ferns and mosses do not grow flowers. New plants grow from tiny spores instead of seeds.

▷ Toadstools are not plants. They are called fungi. Fungi have no roots, leaves or stems. Many fungi are poisonous.

Never touch, pick or eat a toadstool.

Find out more

Conservation
Desert
Farming
Flowers
Forests
Fossils
Grasslands
Mountains
Soil
Trees
Water

Prehistoric life

Earth is thousands of millions of years old. When it was first formed, there was no life at all. The first animals grew in the sea. Since then, millions of different kinds of animals have lived on Earth. We know what some of them looked like from the fossils of their remains.

Earth was formed 4,600 million years ago.

△ Ichthyostega was one of the very first amphibians. It lived on land and water.

▽ Dinosaurs died out 65 million years ago. Since life began on Earth, millions of animals have died out to be replaced by new animals.

▷ Pteraspis was one of the earliest kinds of fish. Fish were the first animals to have backbones.

Pteraspis (Ter-**ah**-spiss)

▽ The land was covered with thick forests about 300 million years ago.

▷ Dinosaurs were not active at night, which meant mammals could come out to hunt. Dinosaurs were cold-blooded animals and needed the sun to provide energy for their bodies.

Find out more

Amphibians
Birds
Dinosaurs
Fish
Fossils
Mammals
Reptiles

Queens

A queen is a woman who rules a country or a kingdom. Sometimes the wife or mother of a king is also called a queen. Queens usually become rulers when their father or mother dies. In some countries women cannot rule at all, in others they can only become queen if they have no brothers.

Penny Black

◁ The first stamp in the world had the head of Queen Victoria on it. It was called the Penny Black.

△ Queen Beatrix is Queen of the Netherlands. Like most queens today, she visits many towns and cities to meet and talk to the people.

▷ Cleopatra was a famous queen who ruled Ancient Egypt. She was very beautiful and clever. She is famous for killing herself with a snake bite.

◁ Elizabeth I was one of the most popular queens of England. She made England rich and powerful.

Find out more

Kings
History

Religion

There are many religions around the world and the people who follow them have different beliefs and customs. Most religions have a god or gods and have rules to tell people how to live together. People who follow a religion may say prayers in a special building and have a priest to guide them. The most popular religions in the world are Christianity, Islam, Hinduism, Buddhism, Sikhism and Judaism.

church

△ Many people worship in special buildings. They may pray in a church, like this one, a mosque, a temple or a synagogue.

Christians
These Christians are celebrating Easter Sunday. They believe that Jesus, the Son of God, died on the cross and came back to life at Easter. They follow his teachings that are written in the New Testament of the Bible.

Sikhs
The Golden Temple at Amritsar in India is the most important holy place where Sikhs go to pray. Sikhs believe in one God and follow the teachings of gurus. They are taught to lead good, simple lives.

Hindus
Every year Hindus celebrate Divali, the festival of lights, to bring good fortune. They worship many gods and believe the soul is re-born after death.

Jews
Candles are lit in a special candlestick during the Jewish festival of Hanukkah. Jews believe in God and their teachings and laws are written in the Bible.

Buddhists

Buddhists say their prayers in front of statues of Buddha, like this one. They follow the teachings of an Indian prince who became known as Buddha.

Muslims

Followers of Islam are called Muslims. These Muslims are praying in the holy city of Mecca. They believe in one God, called Allah, whose words were written down by Muhammad in the Koran.

Other religions

There are many other religions each with their own festivals. Some worship the spirits of natural things, such as trees and rocks. This is a fishing festival in Japan.

Find out more

Asia
Books
Dance
Europe
History
North America
South America

Reptiles

Lizards, crocodiles, turtles and snakes are all reptiles. Some reptiles live in water and some live on land.

Most reptiles live in warm countries. Reptiles that live in cold places sleep through the winter. This is called hibernation. They wake up in the spring when the weather is warmer.

△ Most snakes lay eggs with soft, leathery shells. The young snakes hatch when the eggs are warmed by the heat of the Sun.

gecko

△ A gecko is a lizard with sticky pads on its toes. The pads allow it to run upside down across a ceiling.

Nile crocodile

◁ A crocodile mother looks after her young. When the babies hatch, their mother carries them carefully to the water in her enormous mouth.

Fact box

- All reptiles are cold-blooded. This means that they have to lie in the sun to warm up before they can move around. If their bodies get too hot they have to cool down in the shade.
- Reptiles have dry, scaly skin.
- Dinosaurs were reptiles. The word dinosaur means terrible lizard.

frilled lizard

▷ The frilled lizard spreads its collar and hisses loudly to frighten away enemies.

green turtle

◁ A turtle swims using its strong flippers. It lives in the sea, but it lays its eggs on the seashore.

▽ Many snakes have stretchy jaws, so they can open their mouths very wide. Some snakes can eat a large animal by swallowing it whole.

egg-eating snake

▷ The tortoise lives on land. It pulls its head and legs into its shell if it is scared.

tortoise

▽ The anaconda is a huge snake. It coils its body around its prey and squeezes it to death.

caiman

anaconda

▽ A Komodo dragon is the largest lizard. It can grow up to three and a half metres long. It attacks deer and pigs.

Komodo dragon

Find out more
Animals
Dinosaurs
Prehistoric life

Roads

Roads link one place to another. Cars, buses and lorries travel on roads. Very large roads are called motorways. They have no crossroads or roundabouts, so traffic can travel a long way without stopping. Signs and markings on roads tell drivers which way to go and how fast to travel.

△ Bridges and flyovers help traffic to travel more quickly around crowded cities. Some roads go underground, through tunnels.

How a road is made

▷ Bulldozers shovel away trees and earth.

bulldozer

scraper

◁ Scrapers make the ground level and smooth out a path. Scrapers are pulled by very large tractors.

dumptruck

grader

◁ Dumptrucks bring crushed rock. Graders smooth this in place to make a flat base for the road.

roller

paving machine

△ A paving machine spreads on a mixture of stones, sand and tar, called asphalt. This is then rolled.

Find out more

Conservation

Energy

Maps

Science

Scientists study the world around us. Biologists study living things, geologists study the Earth and astronomers study the stars and planets. All scientists look at things and try to explain what they see. They set up experiments to test their ideas. Scientists discover new things all the time.

△ A microscope makes things look much larger. Scientists use all sorts of tools to help them understand the world around us.

◁ You can be a scientist too. These children are doing an experiment. First they guess which objects might float and which will sink. They sort them into piles.

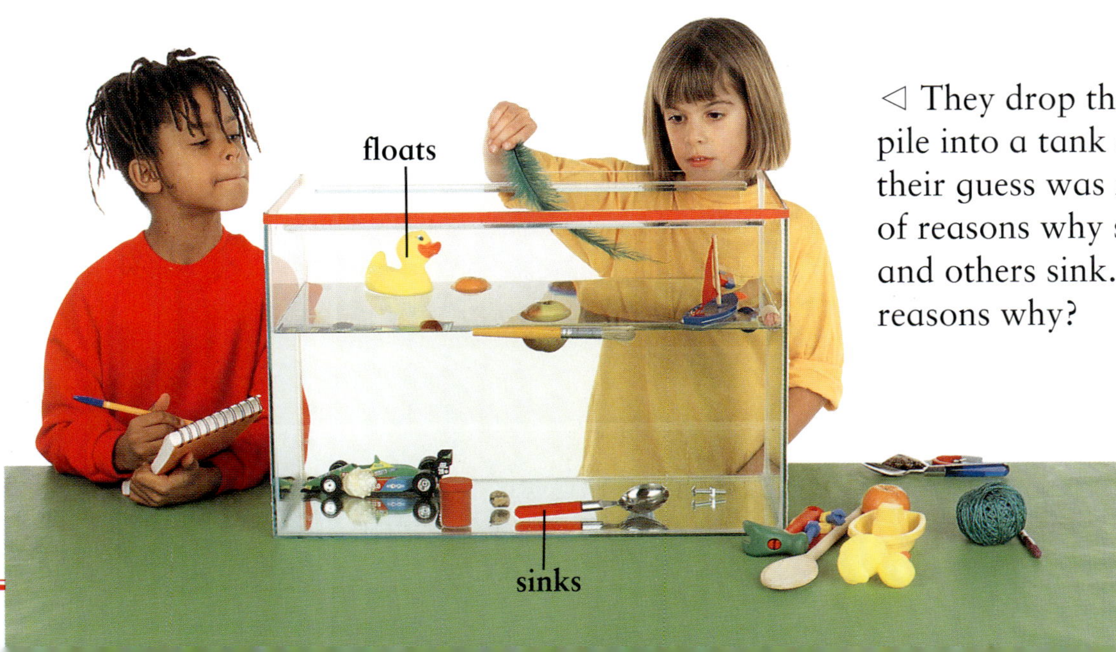

◁ They drop the things from each pile into a tank of water to see if their guess was right. They think of reasons why some objects float and others sink. Do you know the reasons why?

Find out more

Antarctica and Arctic

Electricity

Seashore

The seashore is where the land meets the sea. Some seashores are sandy, others may be rocky, muddy or pebbly. Many different animals and plants live there. The seashore changes its shape all the time. This is because the waves pound against the cliffs and beaches, slowly wearing them away.

△ Twice a day the sea comes high up the shore. This is called high tide.

△ The sea also falls back again twice every day. This is called low tide.

▽ Many seabirds live on the cliffs at the seaside. Puffins nest in burrows at the top. Gannets nest at the top of the cliff too and on ledges below.

◁ Playing on the beach can be great fun. Sand is made up of very tiny pieces of broken rock and shell.

Always use sun cream and a hat to shade yourself from the sun's harmful rays.

Find out more
Animals
Birds
Caves
Europe
Fossils
Oceans and Seas

Seasons

Many parts of the world have four seasons. They are spring, summer, autumn and winter. This is because the Earth is tilted as it travels around the Sun. As the Earth circles the Sun, either the northern half or the southern half of the world leans towards the Sun.

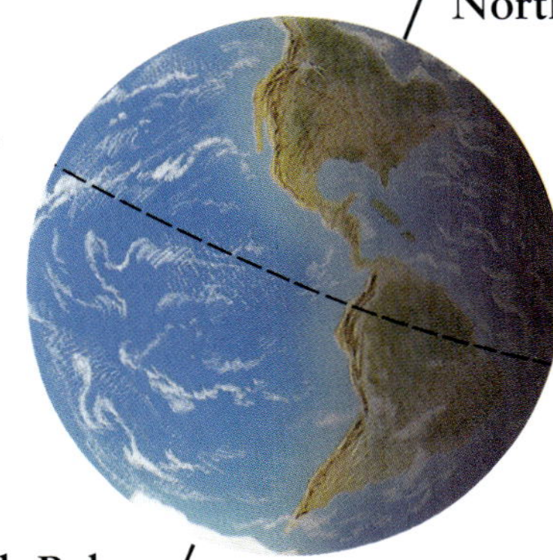

△ It is summer in the southern part of the world when it faces the Sun. In the northern part it is winter.

◁ Spring follows winter. The days become longer and warmer. Plants begin to grow and many animals have babies.

◁ Summer is the warmest season. Flowers bloom and fruits ripen in the sunshine. It does not get dark until late.

◁ In autumn the days get shorter. The weather turns cooler. Trees may lose their leaves. Some birds fly to warmer places.

◁ Winter is the coldest season. It gets dark early in the evening. Plants stop growing and many trees are bare.

△ It is always hot near the Equator. Often there is a dry season and a wet season.

Find out more

Antarctica and Arctic
Birds
Plants
Trees
Weather

Ships and boats

Boats have been used for thousands of years to carry people and goods across water. The first boats were rafts, made from logs or reeds tied together. Boats use sails, oars or engines to push them through the water. Large, sea-going boats are called ships. There are many different kinds of ships and boats.

△ Long ago, the people of Polynesia explored the Pacific Ocean in boats like canoes. They were searching for new islands.

▷ Huge passenger ships are called cruise liners. They are like floating hotels. The parts of a ship all have names. The front is called the bow and the back is called the stern.

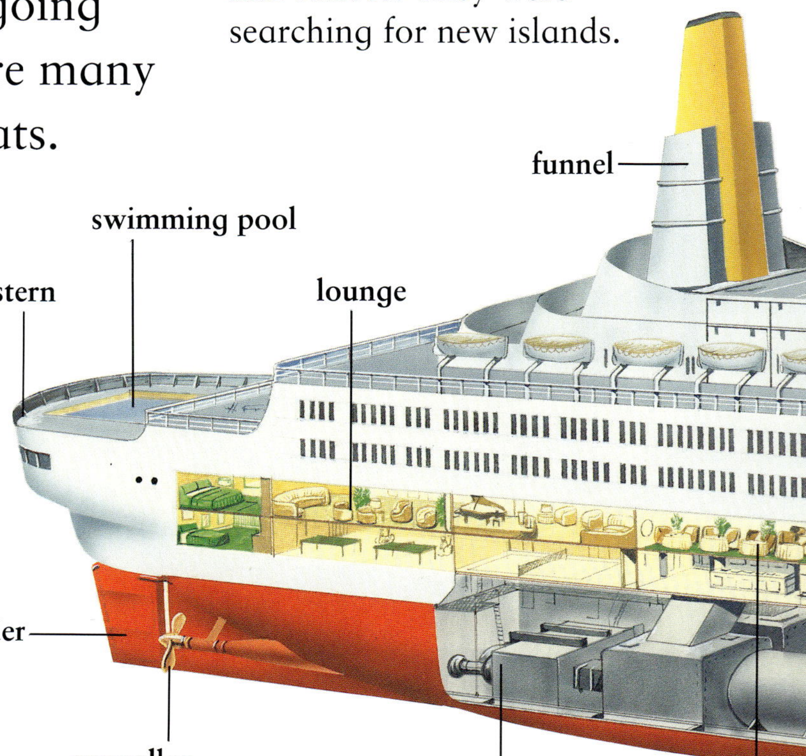

Viking longship

△ The Vikings were great sailors. They built strong, wooden ships, called longboats, which had square sails. They could also row their ships through the water with oars.

kayak

▽ A kayak is a small boat, like a canoe. A paddle is used to push the kayak through the water.

▷ A speed boat has a powerful engine. The front lifts up so it can skim quickly across the top of the water.

speed boat

▽ A racing yacht has a large sail at the front, called the spinnaker. When it catches the wind, the yacht races along the sea.

racing yacht

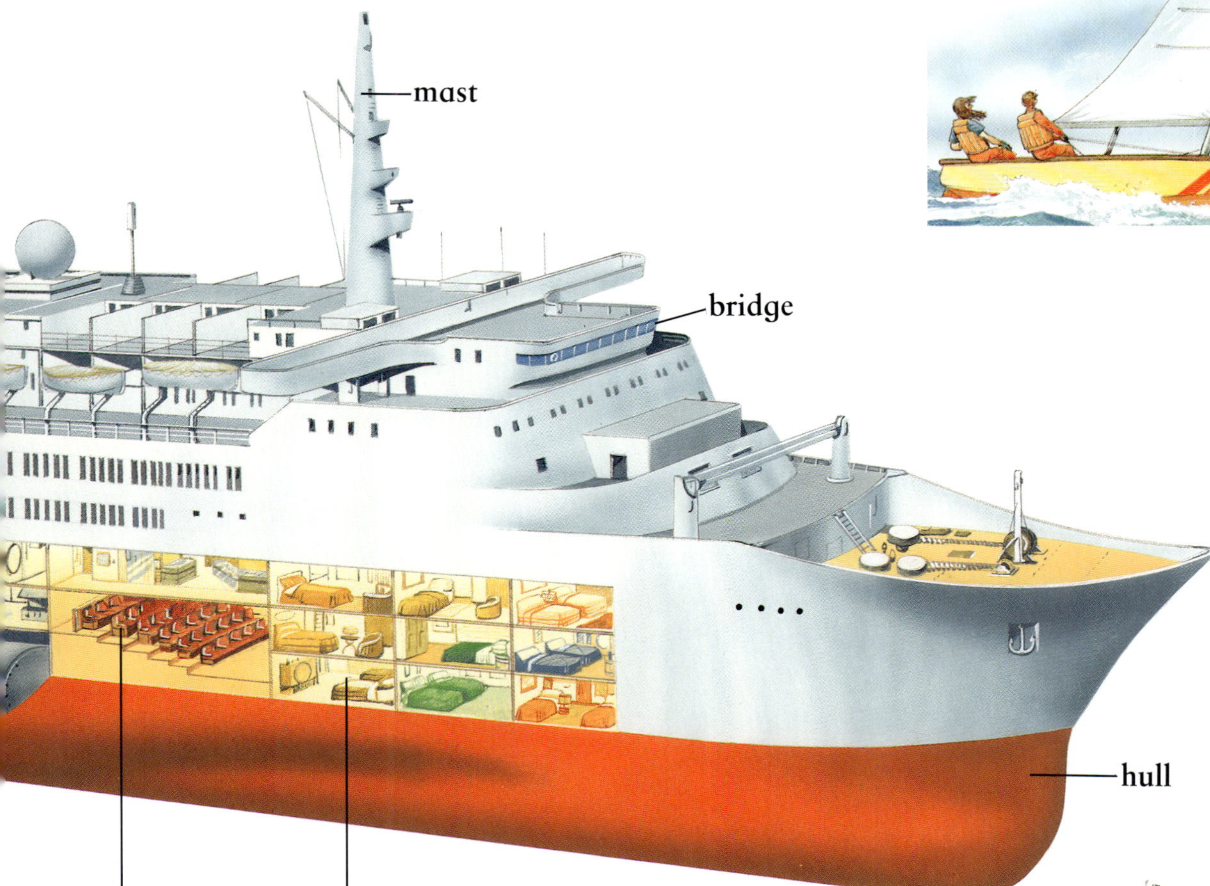

cruise liner

▷ The biggest ships in the world are oil tankers. They can be half a kilometre long and so heavy that they take 20 minutes to stop.

oil tanker

Find out more

Conservation
Fishing
History
Religion
Science
South America

Soil

The soil beneath your feet is made up of tiny bits of rock mixed with tiny pieces of plants. It is full of life. Hundreds of beetles, worms, slugs and other even smaller things live there. Plants get their water and other important things that they need in order to grow from the soil.

Always wash your hands after you have played with soil.

△ To find out what soil is made up of, shake some up in a jar of water and leave it to settle. The soil will settle in layers of different material.

soil after two days

▽ Many animals live in the ground. The roots of trees and grass stop the soil being blown or washed away.

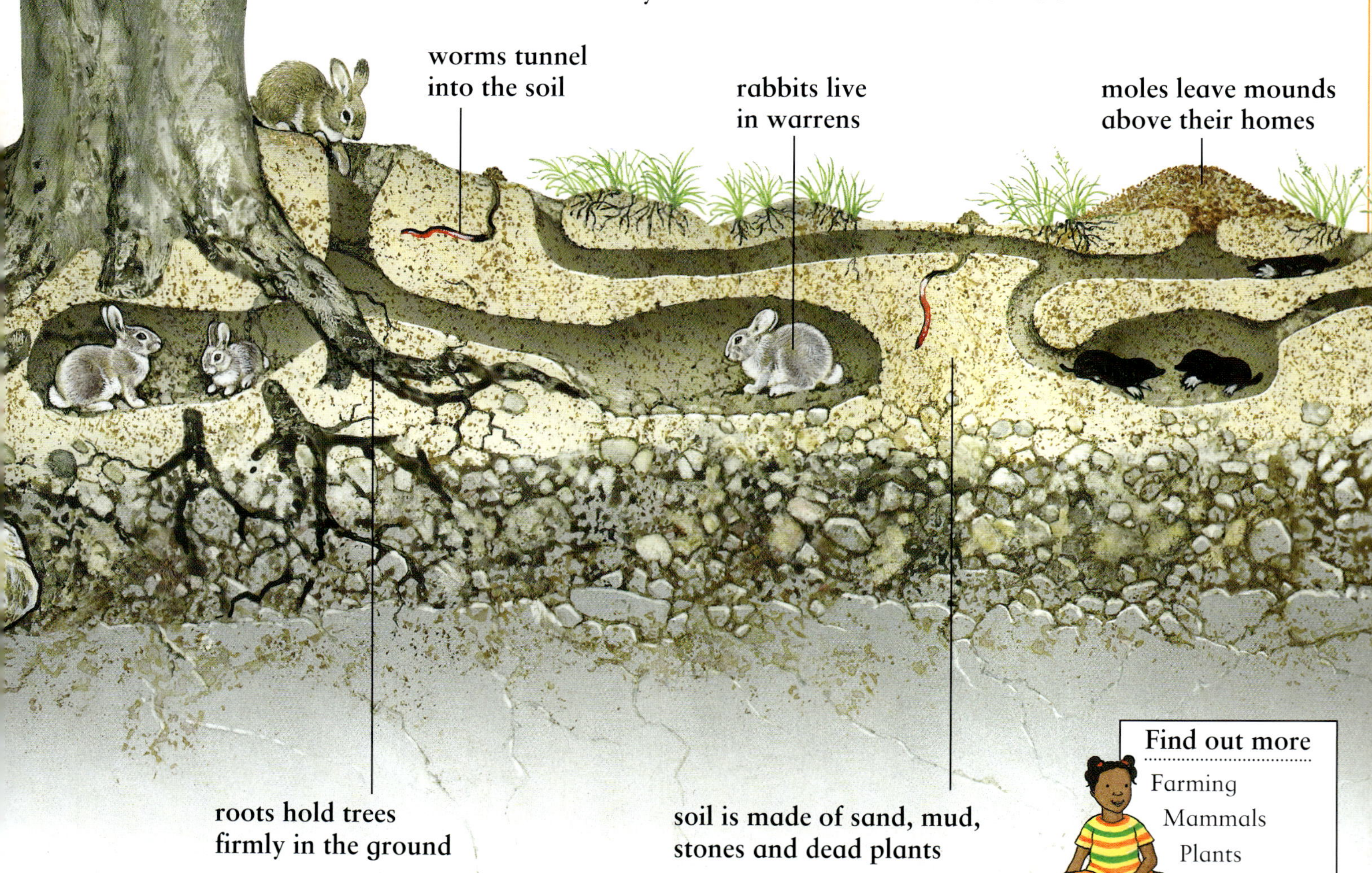

Find out more

Farming
Mammals
Plants

Sound

Sounds are made when something moves backwards and forwards very quickly. This is called vibration. Every single noise you hear is made by something vibrating. Sound is invisible and moves in waves through the air. Sound waves can also travel through a liquid, like water, or a solid, like glass.

Concorde

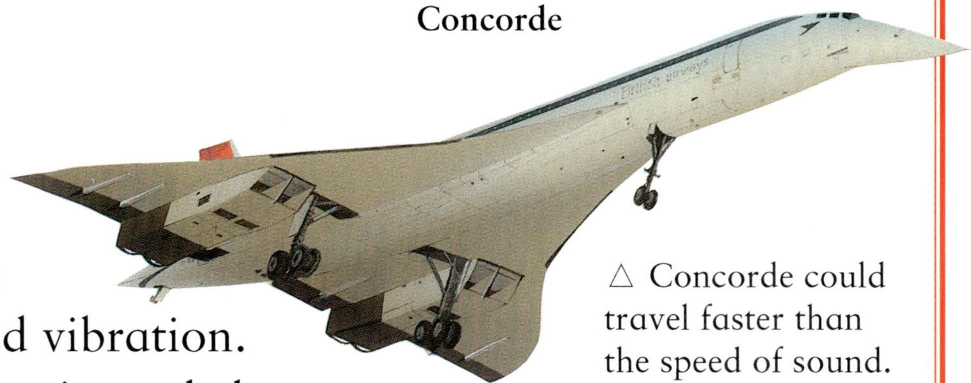

△ Concorde could travel faster than the speed of sound. It is called a supersonic aeroplane.

sound waves

△ You hear sounds when sound waves reach your ears. Inside each ear you have an ear-drum. Sound waves hit your ear-drums and make them vibrate.

▷ When something vibrates very fast, like this whistle, it makes a high sound. Things that vibrate more slowly, such as the double bass, make a lower sound.

whistle

double bass

Find out more

Energy
Flying machines
Human body
Inventions
Music

South America

South America is the fourth largest continent. Down one side runs a long line of mountains called the Andes. The world's largest rainforest grows around the Amazon River. It has hot and cold deserts and large grassy plains. Many of South America's people live in crowded cities and are very poor.

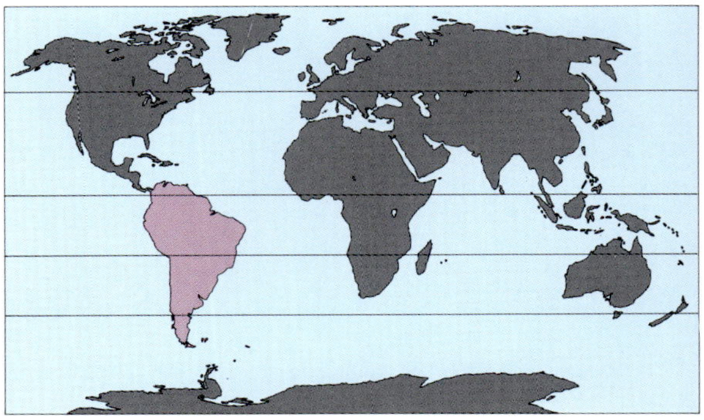

△ South America is shown in purple. It is joined to North America by a thin stretch of land.

▷ The people who live around Lake Titicaca, in the Andes, build their boats and houses out of reeds.

◁ Statues and ruins are all that is left of the ancient cities of South America. This statue is from a city called Tiahuanaco.

▷ Llamas are kept for their meat and wool and are used to carry heavy goods up mountain roads.

▷ Cowboys, called gauchos, look after enormous herds of cattle on the grassy plains of Argentina. The grasslands are called the pampas.

▽ Angel Falls, in the thick rainforest of Venezuela, is the highest waterfall in the world.

▷ Macaws live in the lush Amazon rainforest. Snakes, monkeys and big cats also live there.

scarlet macaw

◁ Above the city of Rio de Janeiro stands a huge statue of Christ. Rio is the main port of Brazil. Its beautiful bay is surrounded by mountains.

Find out more
Conservation
Grasslands
World

Space exploration

To find out more about the planets and stars, rockets are used to carry people and objects into Space. People who travel into Space are called astronauts. They have to wear special suits in Space to survive. Spacecraft are machines that can travel into Space. One of the best known is the Space Shuttle.

▽ The Space Shuttle can carry up to seven astronauts into Space. Its doors open up in Space to release its cargo of scientific instruments. An astronaut controls a robot arm to move the cargo.

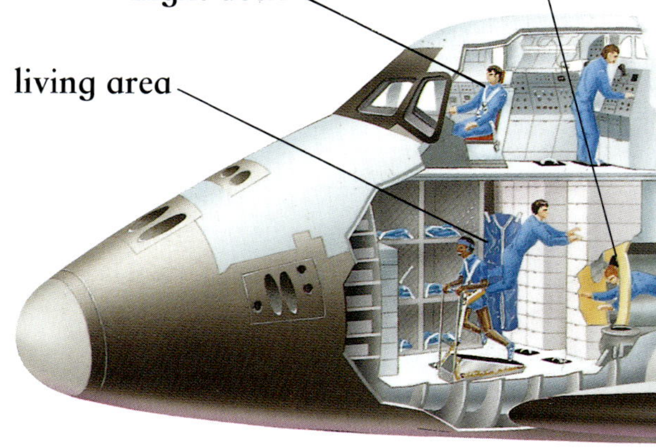

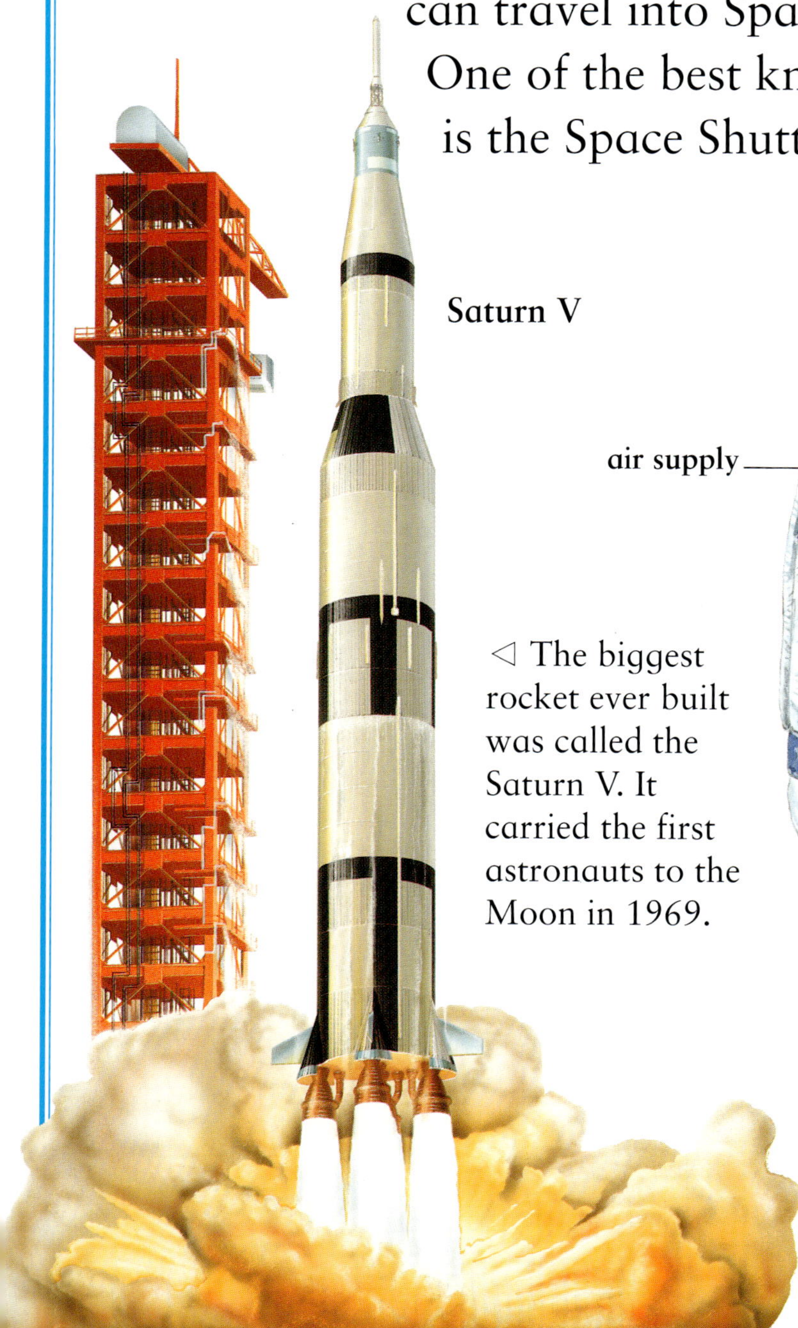

◁ The biggest rocket ever built was called the Saturn V. It carried the first astronauts to the Moon in 1969.

◁ There is no air to breathe in Space. Astronauts wear spacesuits for protection to work outside their spacecraft.

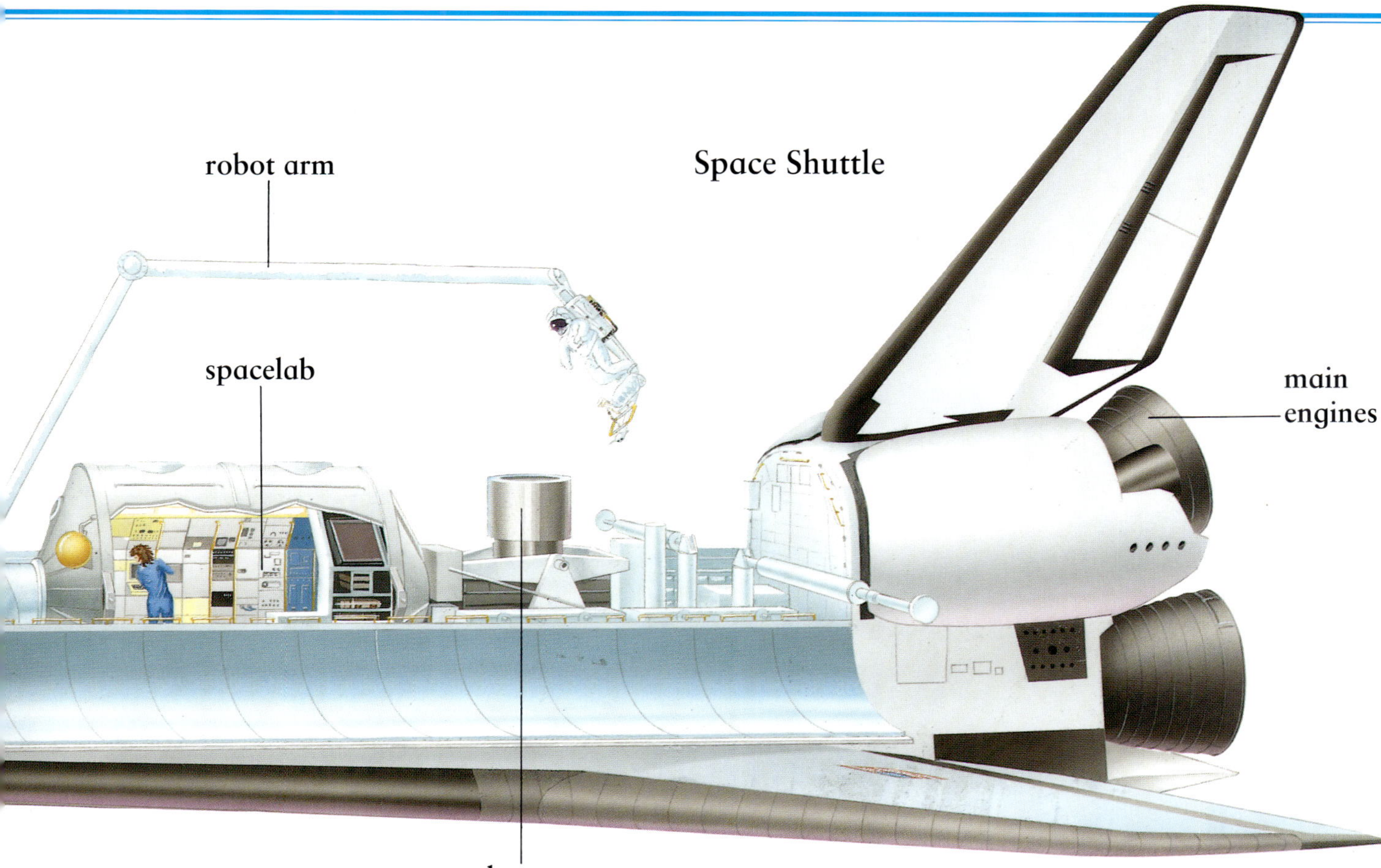

◁ The Space Shuttle takes off with a huge fuel tank and two booster rockets to blast it into Space. It takes only a few minutes for it to travel into Space.

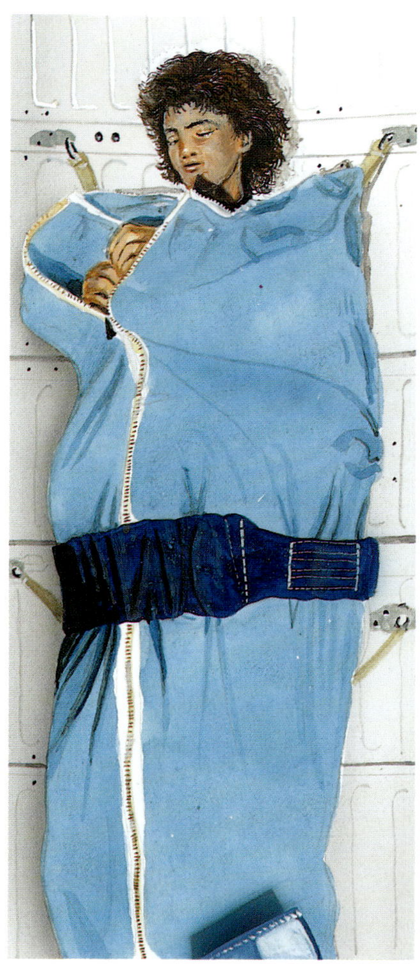

◁ In Space nothing has any weight. Astronauts have to move around carefully. They are strapped into their sleeping bags to stop them floating around.

Satellites and probes
Rockets also carry satellites and probes into Space. These machines send back information to Earth.

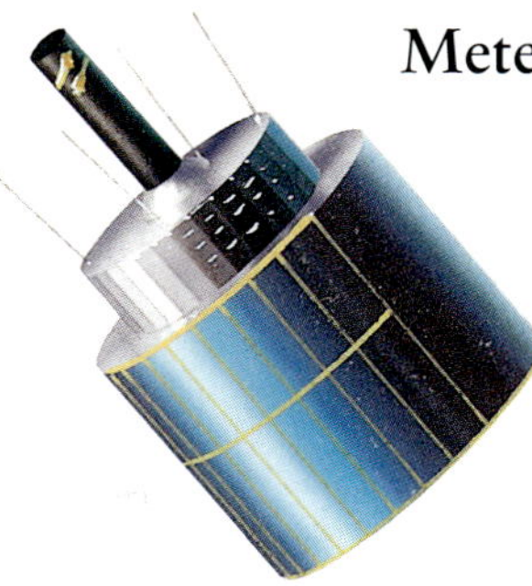

Meteosat

△ Meteosat watches weather patterns. It sends information to computers on Earth.

▷ The giant Hubble Space Telescope sends back pictures of stars and galaxies to astronomers on Earth.

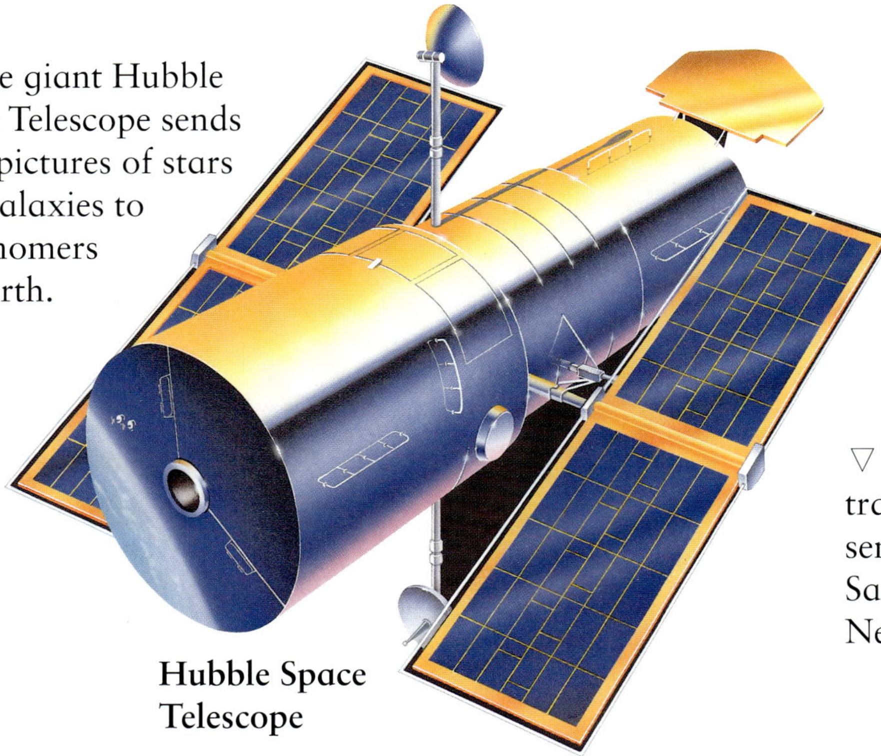

Hubble Space Telescope

▽ Voyager 2 was a probe that travelled out to the planets. It sent back pictures of Jupiter, Saturn, Uranus and Neptune.

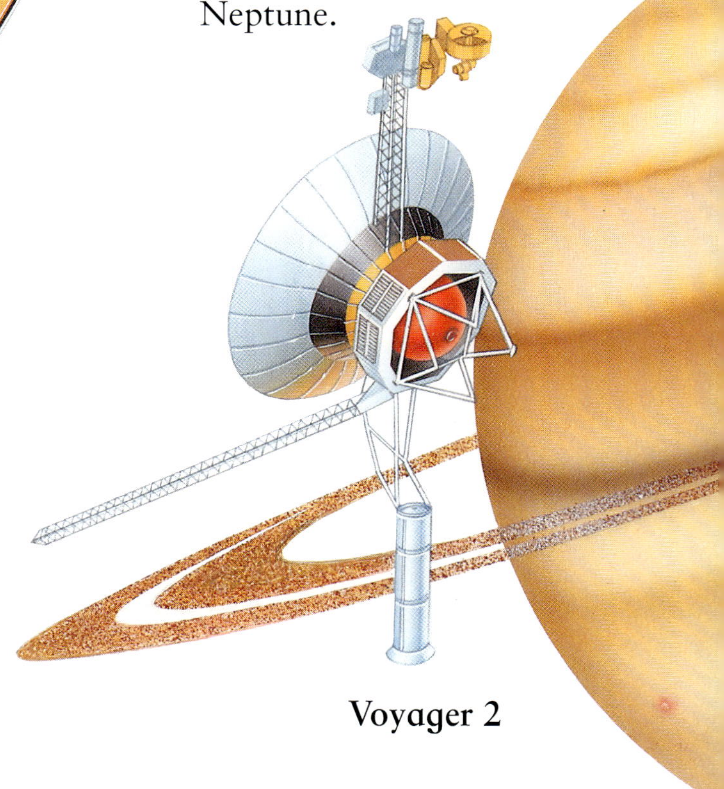

Voyager 2

◁ These astronauts are mending a broken satellite. The satellite has been taken into the Space Shuttle's repair bay.

Find out more
Inventions
Moon
Universe

Spiders

Spiders have eight legs. They feed mainly on insects. Most spiders spin sticky webs of silk to trap their prey. Some go hunting or lie in wait for prey to pass by. Spiders kill their prey by biting them with poisonous fangs.

bird-eating spider

△ This big bird-eating spider lives in the South American rainforest. It sometimes catches birds on nests, but usually eats insects that it hunts at night.

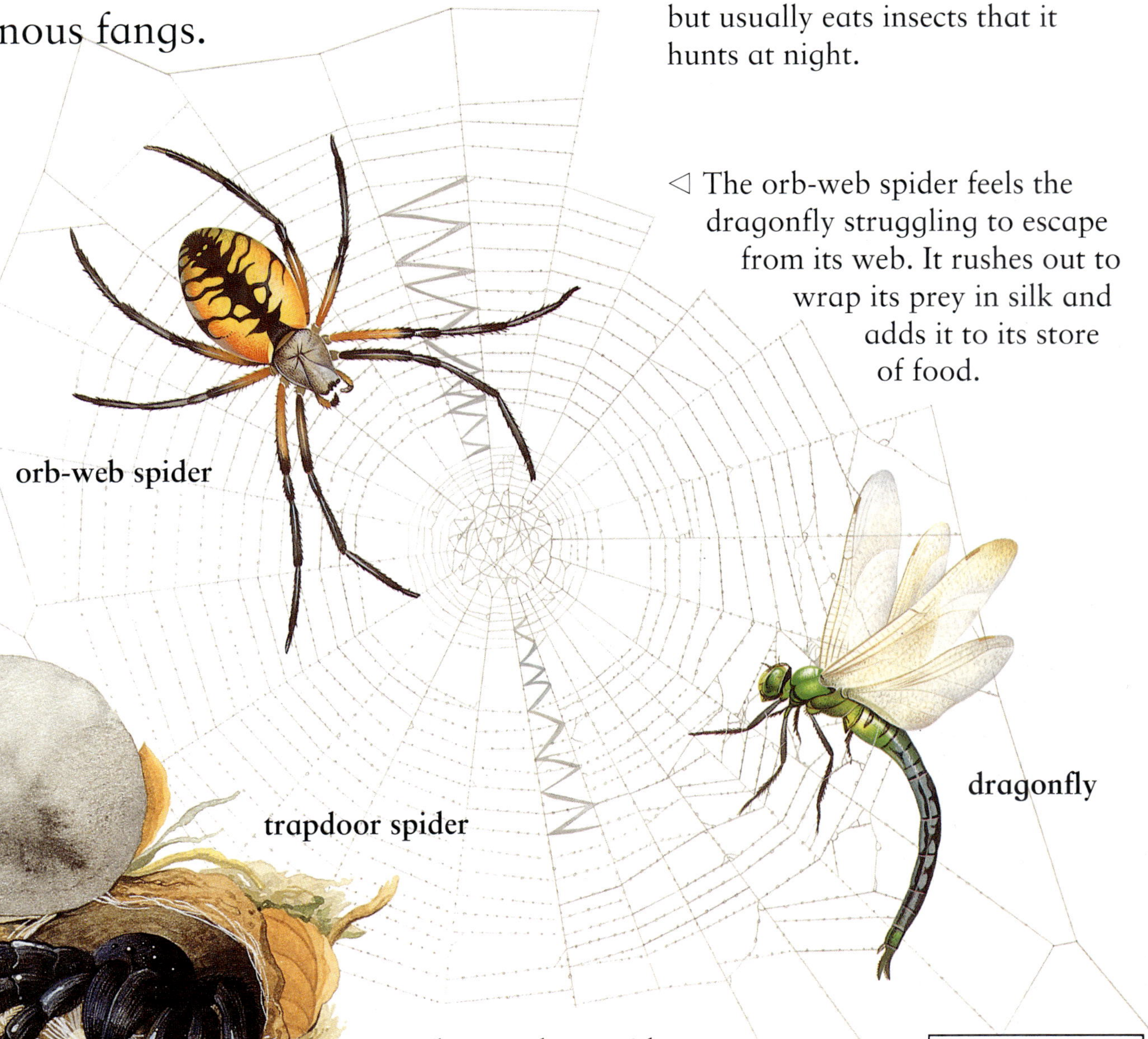

orb-web spider

dragonfly

◁ The orb-web spider feels the dragonfly struggling to escape from its web. It rushes out to wrap its prey in silk and adds it to its store of food.

trapdoor spider

◁ The trapdoor spider hunts by hiding behind a trapdoor in its burrow. When it hears an insect outside, it jumps out and pounces on it.

Find out more
Forests
Stories

Sports

People play sports for many reasons. It may be their job or they may do it just for fun. Sport helps them to stay fit and healthy. Some sports are played by one person. Others are played by two or more people. In many sports two teams compete with each other. Some sports, like horse racing, involve animals as well as people.

△ Football is played all over the world. In some countries it is called soccer. Footballers need great skill to control the ball with their feet.

◁ Gymnasts must learn from a young age how to perform difficult exercises on the floor and on special pieces of equipment, like this one, called the bar.

▷ Baseball is one of the favourite team sports in America. This boy is called the pitcher.

◁ In Mongolia, boys and girls as young as five dress up to take part in horse races.

▷ Ice-hockey is Canada's most popular sport. It is a fast and tough game. Helmets and pads are worn for protection.

▽ When two people play tennis against each other it is called singles. When four play it is called doubles.

△ Swimmers train hard to swim fast. They learn different strokes, called breaststroke, backstroke, front crawl and butterfly.

▷ The Olympic Games are held every four years. Countries send their best athletes to compete.

Find out more

Cars
Clothes
Health
Human body
Mountains
Oceans and seas

Stories

Stories tell you about events. Some stories are about real things, others are made up. Long ago, people told each other stories about their gods or about real people who had done amazing things. Now we read stories in books, comics or watch them in films and on television.

△ The Aboriginal people of Australia paint stories to tell how the land was made.

▽ Use your imagination to write and illustrate your own story. Make it a scary, funny or magical story. Draw pictures of the characters.

▷ In Ancient Greece, stories were told about a winged horse named Pegasus. He was caught by Bellerophon and did many brave deeds.

◁ In Ghana, in Africa, people tell stories about a spider called Anansi who likes to play tricks.

▷ Comic strips tell stories with pictures. The words people say are written in speech bubbles.

▷ Jack and the Beanstalk is a folk tale. Jack climbs a huge beanstalk to steal a magic hen from a wicked and cruel giant.

◁ The story of the Wizard of Oz was made into a famous film. Dorothy helps a scarecrow, a lion and a tin man.

Find out more

- Africa
- Art and artists
- Books
- Dance
- Drama

Sun

The Sun is a star. It is a dazzling ball of burning gases. The Sun is the nearest, most important star to the Earth. It gives us light and warmth. Earth is just the right distance from the Sun. If Earth was closer to the Sun it would burn up. If it was farther away it would be freezing cold.

△ During an eclipse the Moon hides the Sun. This is the only time we see clouds of white gas, called the corona, that surround the Sun.

Never look straight at the Sun. It will damage your eyes.

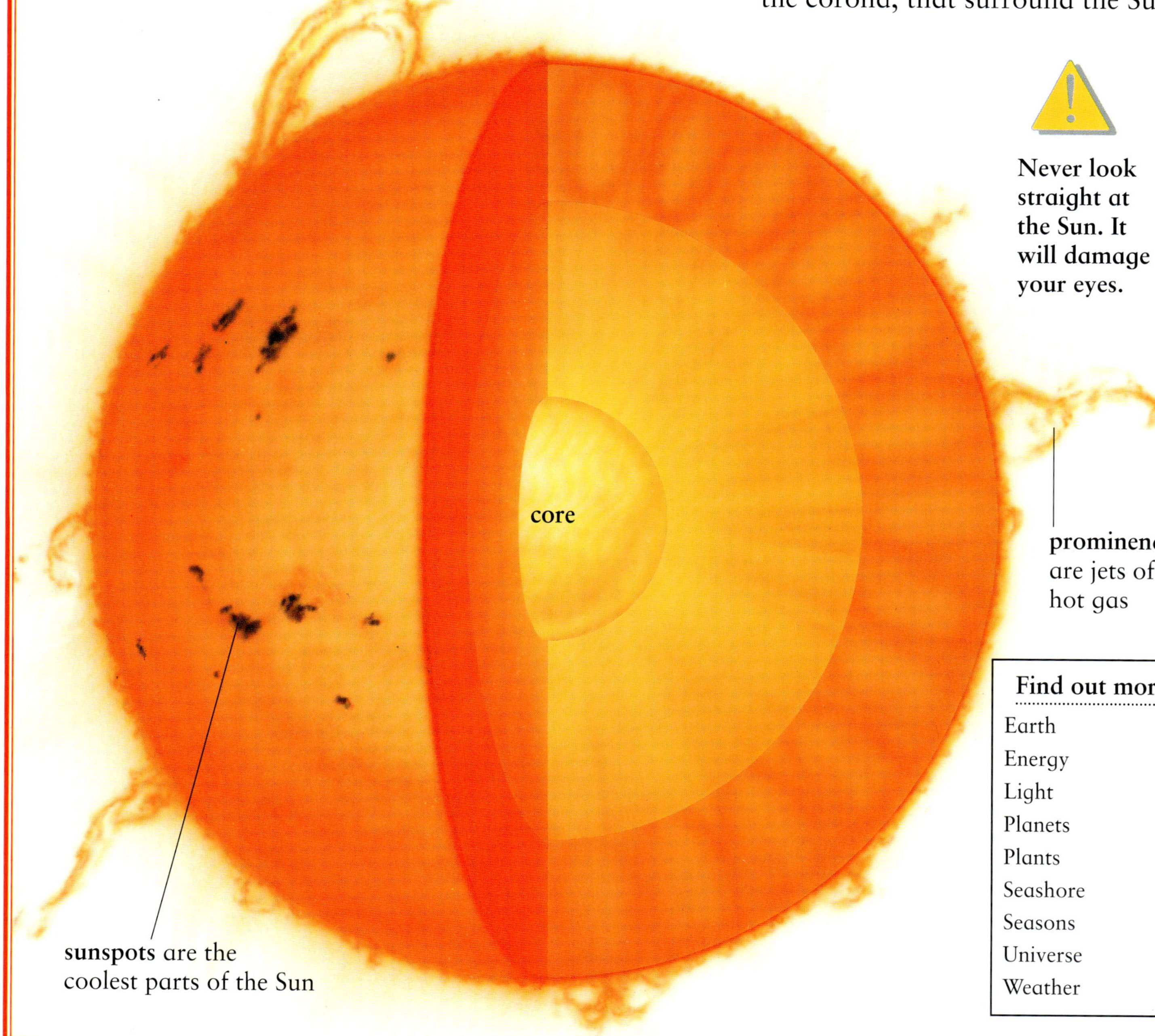

prominences are jets of hot gas

sunspots are the coolest parts of the Sun

Find out more

Earth
Energy
Light
Planets
Plants
Seashore
Seasons
Universe
Weather

Time

We use clocks and watches to measure time exactly in hours, minutes and seconds. Before clocks and watches were invented people measured time roughly in days, nights and seasons. Later people used candle clocks and shadow clocks, which were not as accurate as the clocks we have today.

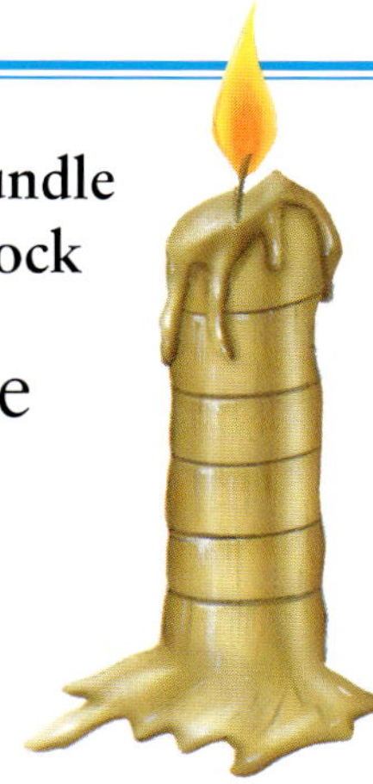

candle clock

◁ Candle clocks were marked in sections. The candle burned away one section every hour. People could tell the time by the number of sections left.

video machine

△ This video recorder has a digital clock. It uses the clock to start a recording at the right time.

alarm clock

△ An alarm clock can be set to wake you up in time for something. Many children need alarm clocks to wake them up in time for school.

stopwatch

△ This boy uses a stopwatch to time his friend running a race. He stops the watch when his friend crosses over the finishing line.

Find out more

Earth
Machines
Moon
Seasons
Year

Trains

All over the world, trains pull heavy loads along rails. The rails make it easier for the wheels to turn. The first trains used steam engines to drive the wheels. Now, most trains run on electricity or diesel fuel. Trains carry people and goods for long distances, at high speeds.

steam train

△ Steam trains were invented 200 years ago. They used coal or wood to make steam to drive the wheels.

◁ Train tunnels are made by huge drills called TBMs (tunnel-boring machines). They cut through the rock and soil.

tunnel-boring machine

△ Many overcrowded cities have underground trains. The trains run on electrified rails and carry people through tunnels under the city.

coal wagon

flatcar

diesel engine

◁ Trains that carry goods are called freight trains. Some can pull over 100 wagons.

TGV

◁ The Japanese Bullet train can travel as fast as 300 km per hour.

Find out more

Electricity
Inventions
Machines

Trees

Trees are plants. They are the largest living things on Earth. Many of them live for hundreds of years.

Trees give food and shelter to birds, insects and many other animals. Mushrooms and other fungi grow on their roots and on dead tree stumps.

△ Each year, a layer of wood grows inside the trunk of a tree and makes a ring. You can tell how old a tree was by counting the number of rings in the trunk.

deciduous

oak tree

maple fruit

maple leaf

oak leaf

oak fruit (acorn)

△ Deciduous trees start to lose their leaves in autumn and have no leaves in winter. They grow new leaves in the spring.

evergreen

spruce tree

spruce cone

monkey-puzzle cones

△ Evergreen trees keep their leaves all year. Many have spiky, needle-like leaves that are not harmed by the cold.

Find out more

Conservation
Flowers
Forests
Mountains
Plants
Prehistoric life
Seasons
Soil

Trucks

Trucks carry all sorts of things in huge containers, called trailers. Many travel long distances from one country to another. Others travel much shorter distances. Some bring food and goods to shops. Others take materials to and from factories. Trucks are also called lorries.

△ This truck is called a road train. Road trains can pull three huge trailers. They are used in Australia.

△ The crane on the back of a logging truck is used to lift logs onto the trailer. This truck is used in places with large forests.

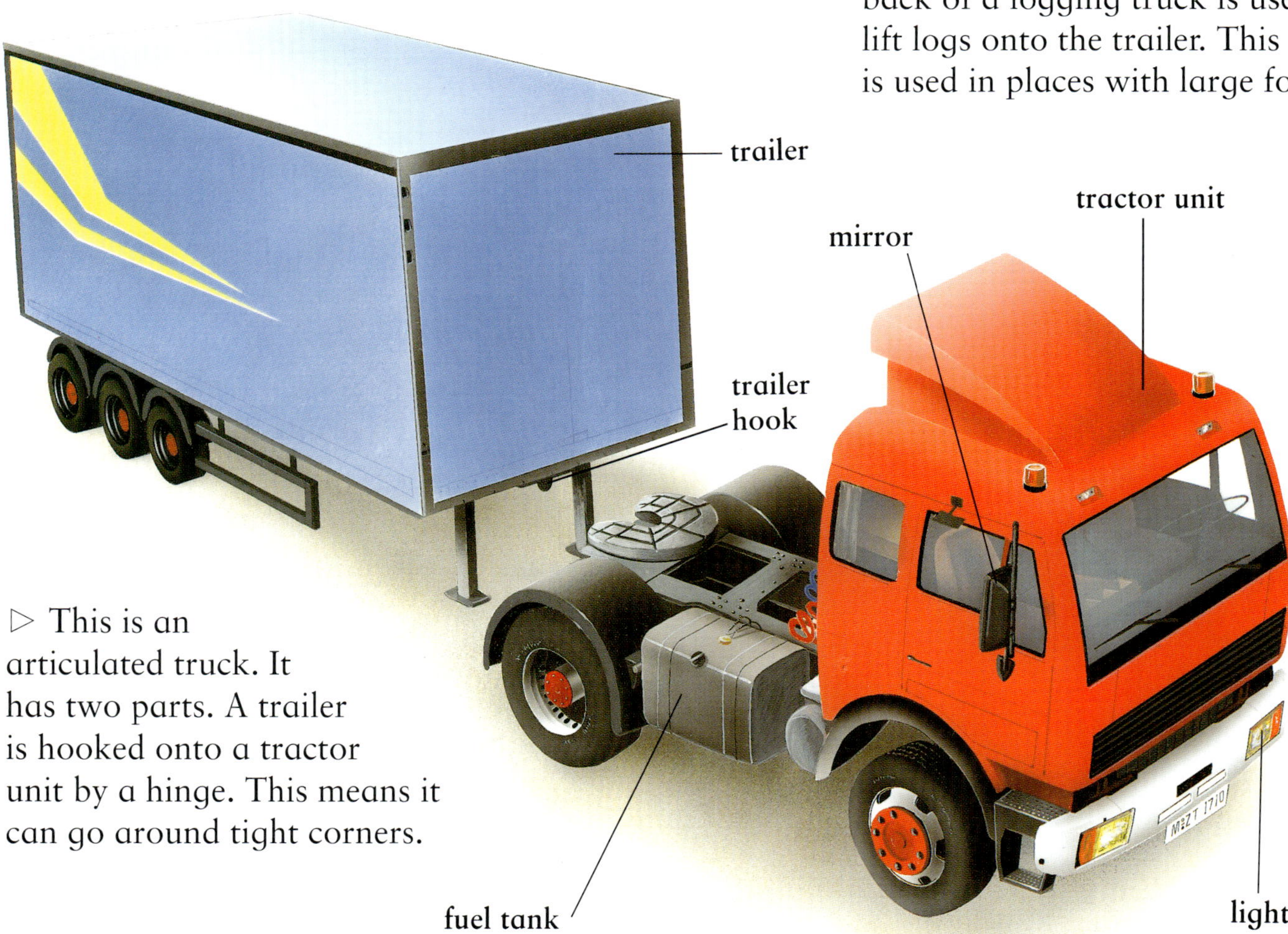

▷ This is an articulated truck. It has two parts. A trailer is hooked onto a tractor unit by a hinge. This means it can go around tight corners.

◁ Small pick-up trucks, like this one, have open backs. They are used all over the world.

Find out more

Conservation
Machines
Roads

Universe

The Earth, the Sun, the Moon and all the planets and stars are all part of the Universe. The Earth is just one planet that circles around our Sun. The Sun and all the stars you can see in the sky at night make up our galaxy, called the Milky Way. The Milky Way is a tiny part of the Universe. Everything, even light, energy, animals and plants, is part of the Universe. It is very hard to imagine how big the Universe really is.

△ Even when you look through a telescope you can only see a tiny part of the Universe.

◁ This picture is of huge groups of stars, called galaxies. It was taken in space by the Hubble Space Telescope.

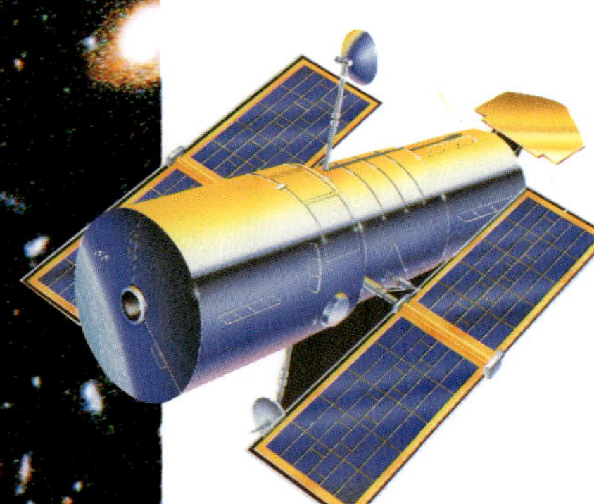

Hubble Space Telescope

The life of a star

New stars are being made all the time. They shine for a very long time and then they die. A red giant is a huge, old star.

Little Bear

Southern Cross

△ Long ago, people gave names to patterns of stars in the sky. These are called constellations. The Little Bear can be seen by people living in northern parts of the world. The Southern Cross can be seen by people living in the south.

1 Stars are born in vast, spinning clouds of dust and gas. A cloud of dust and gas is called a nebula.

2 The gas and dust shrink and join to form lots of balls. These become a cluster of baby stars.

3 As a star gets hotter it begins to shine. Most stars, like our Sun, shine steadily nearly all their lives.

4 Towards the end of its life, the star swells up. It can become as much as 100 times bigger in size. At this stage the star is called a red giant.

5 A red giant shrinks into a white dwarf when it has used up all its fuel. It is still very hot but its size makes it appear very faint.

6 After a very long time, the star cools down and ends its life as a cold, black dwarf star.

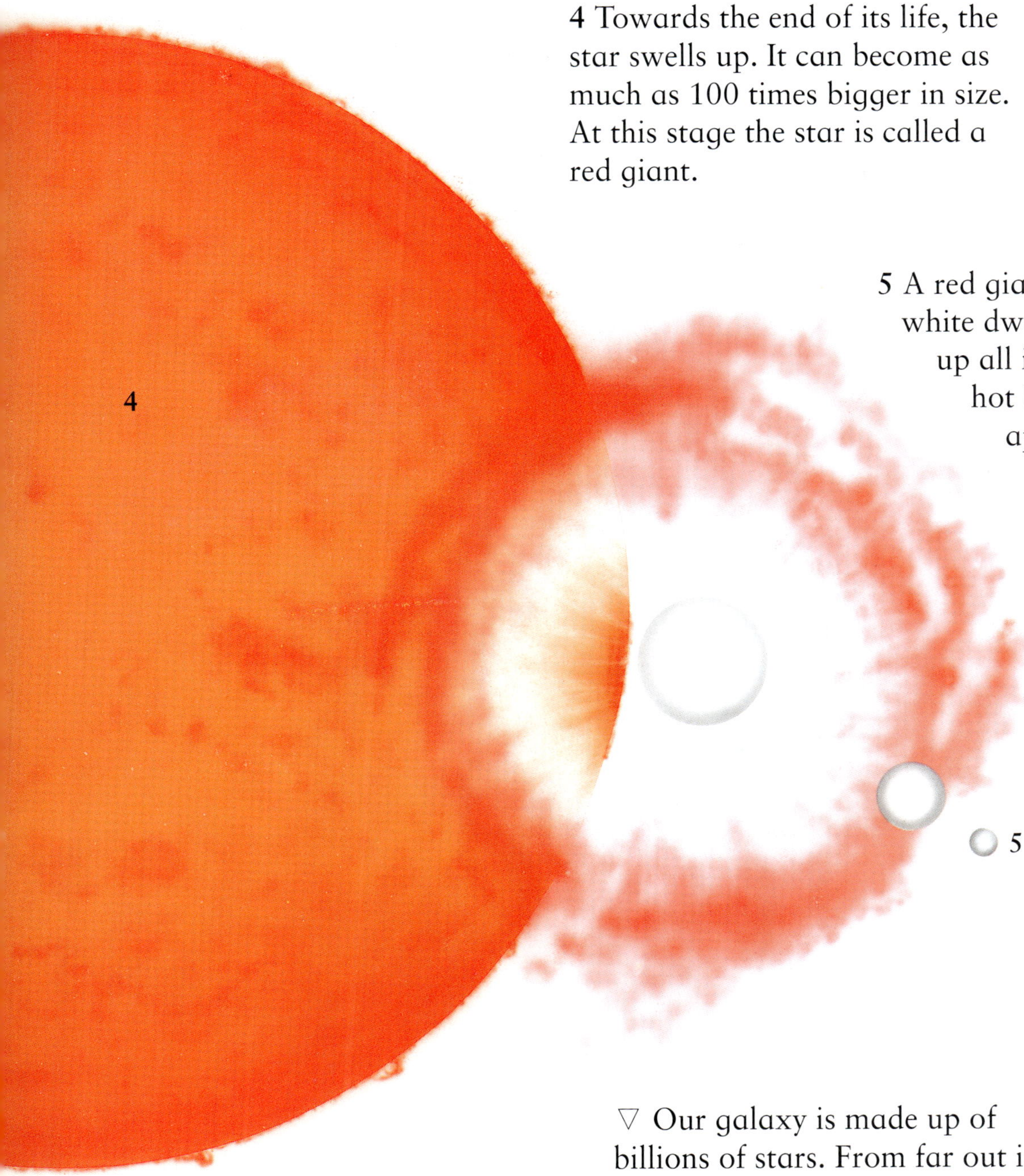

▽ Our galaxy is made up of billions of stars. From far out in Space it would look like a spiral of stars.

Find out more

Earth
Moon
Planets
Space exploration
Sun

Volcano

A volcano is a mountain made of ash and hot, runny rock called lava. Ash and lava spurt out of a crack in the Earth's surface. When the lava cools, it hardens into rock. Volcanoes may erupt once, then not erupt again for many years.

Find out more
Earth
Oceans and seas

Water

All life on Earth needs water. Without it everything would die. Water covers nearly three-quarters of the world. There is salty water in the oceans and seas, and fresh water in lakes, rivers and ponds. Frozen water, or ice, usually covers the oceans around Antarctica and in the Arctic. All these watery places are home to many different plants and animals.

△ A pond skater can walk on water because of a force called surface tension. This force makes a thin stretchy layer on the water.

▷ When water is a liquid it flows and spreads. It fills the container that it is poured into and it has a flat surface.

▷ If water becomes very cold it freezes and turns into solid ice. When ice melts it turns back into water.

▽ When water is very hot it boils. Tiny bubbles rise up, burst and release steam.

▽ Steam cools when it hits something cold and turns into water droplets. This change is called condensation.

How we use water

▷ **1** Water falls as rain and runs into streams and rivers. It is collected and stored in big lakes called reservoirs.

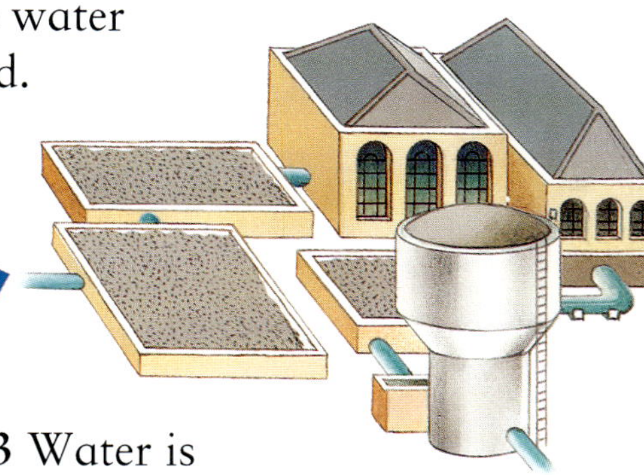

▷ **2** The water is cleaned.

▽ **3** Water is pumped into houses in underground pipes.

△ **4** After it has been used, the water goes down into big pipes called sewers.

△ **5** The water is cleaned before it flows back into a river or the sea.

▽ Plants need water. Their roots soak up water from the soil. The water travels up the stems to the leaves where it helps to make food.

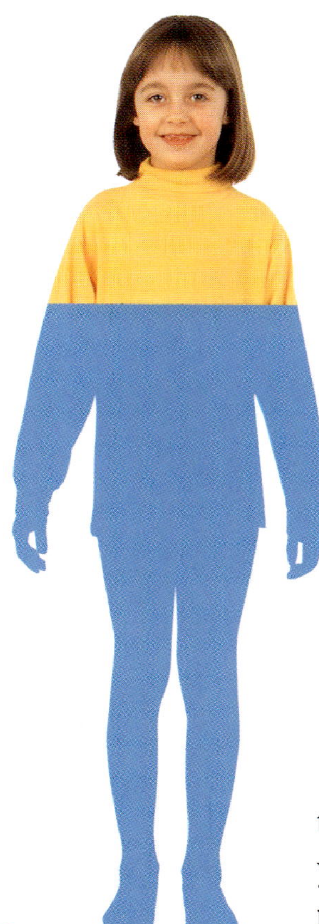

Fact box

- You lose water from your body when you sweat, breathe and go to the toilet.
- You need to drink about one-and-a-half litres of water a day to stay healthy.
- You could not live for more than three days without water.

◁ More than two-thirds of your body is made of water.

◁ In the dry grasslands of Africa, groups of animals gather at the waterhole. They watch out for hungry lions as they take a long drink.

▽ This mangrove swamp is a wet area of land near the sea. Mangrove trees usually have long, strong roots to anchor them in the mud.

◁ A salmon swims from the sea to lay its eggs in the stream where it was born. Some bears wait near waterfalls to catch salmon.

▽ Many different plants grow in and around ponds. They provide food, shelter and nesting places for all sorts of birds, insects and other water creatures.

Find out more

Amphibians
Animals
Caves
Energy
Oceans and seas
Fish
Plants
Science
Seashore
Weather
World

Weather

The weather changes all the time. One day the sky may be clear and sunny, the next it may be cloudy and rainy. Three things cause the weather: air, Sun and water. Air is always on the move and makes the wind. The Sun gives warmth, and the water makes clouds, rain, snow and hail.

▽ This picture shows how the Earth uses its water over and over again. It is called the **water cycle**.

1 Every day, the Sun's heat turns water from seas and lakes into an invisible gas called water vapour.

2 As the air rises, it cools down and the water vapour turns into tiny drops of water or ice crystals.

3 Lots of drops of water join together to make clouds. The wind blows the clouds over the land.

4 Water in the clouds falls as rain, hail, sleet or snow.

5 Rivers carry the water back to the sea.

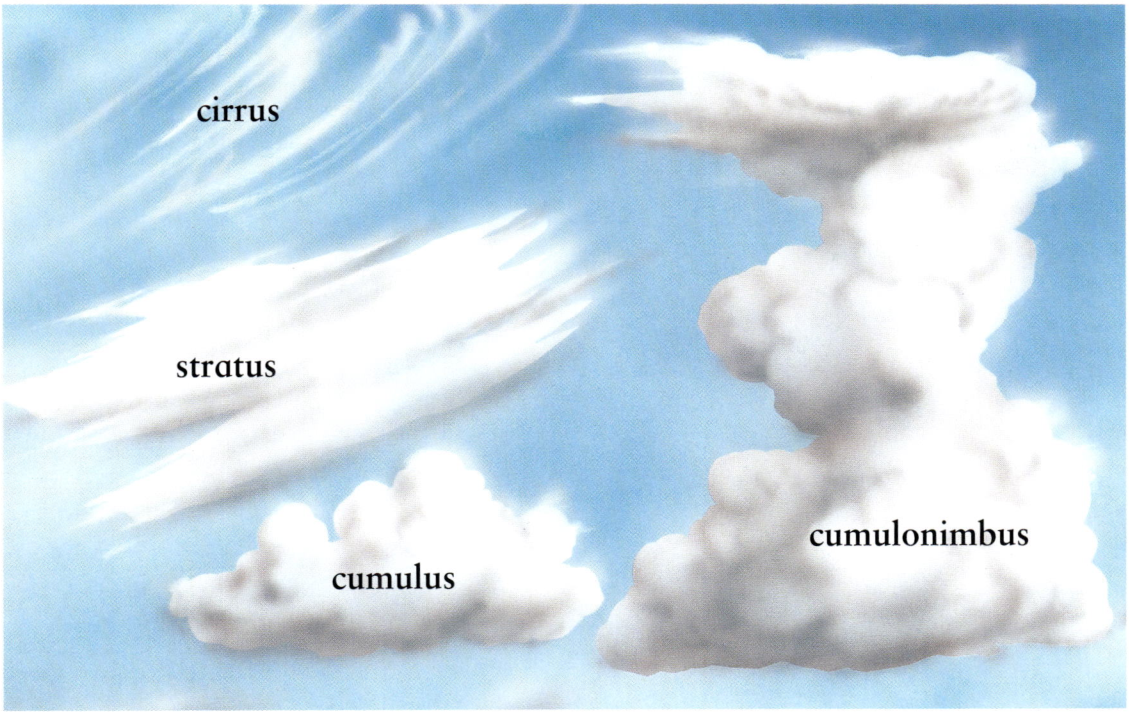

◁ There are different kinds of cloud. Fluffy clouds are called cumulus. Flat clouds are called stratus. Huge cumulonimbus clouds bring storms. Cirrus clouds are high up and wispy.

▷ Snowflakes are water drops that have frozen into ice crystals. No two snowflakes are ever the same.

▽ In very cold places, ice and snow often cover the land for most of the year.

△ Fog and mist are really clouds floating close to the ground. On roads, thick fog makes it difficult for drivers to see where they are going.

△ Thunderstorms start in big black thunderclouds that gather in the sky.

△ Electricity builds up inside the clouds. This causes big sparks of lightning.

△ When lightning flashes, it heats the air and makes a noise. This is thunder.

◁ A tornado is a spinning funnel of wind that speeds across the ground. As it spins, it sucks up rocks, trees and houses in its path.

△ Hailstones are frozen drops of rain. As they blow about inside a cloud, layers of ice form around them until they are heavy enough to fall.

barometer

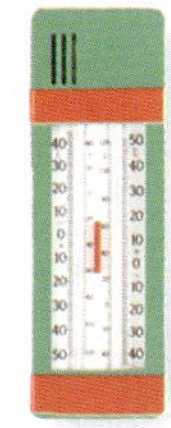

thermometer

▷ A thermometer is an instrument used to measure the temperature of the air. This shows how hot or how cold it is.

△ A barometer is an instrument used to measure the pressure of the air. If the air pressure changes, it usually means that there will be a change in the weather too.

wind vane

△ A wind vane shows which direction the wind is blowing in. Winds that blow from the west are called westerlies. Winds that blow from the north are called northerlies.

◁ A rain gauge is used to measure rainfall. The rain falls through a funnel into a container. A scale shows how much rain has fallen.

rain gauge

Find out more

Air
Clothes
Earth
Energy
Light
Seasons
Space exploration
Sun
Water

World

Most of the world is covered by the sea. Only a third is covered by land. There are seven large areas of land, called continents. People have divided most of them into countries. Each country has its own name, its own government and its own flag. There are about 190 countries in the world. Many different peoples live in each one.

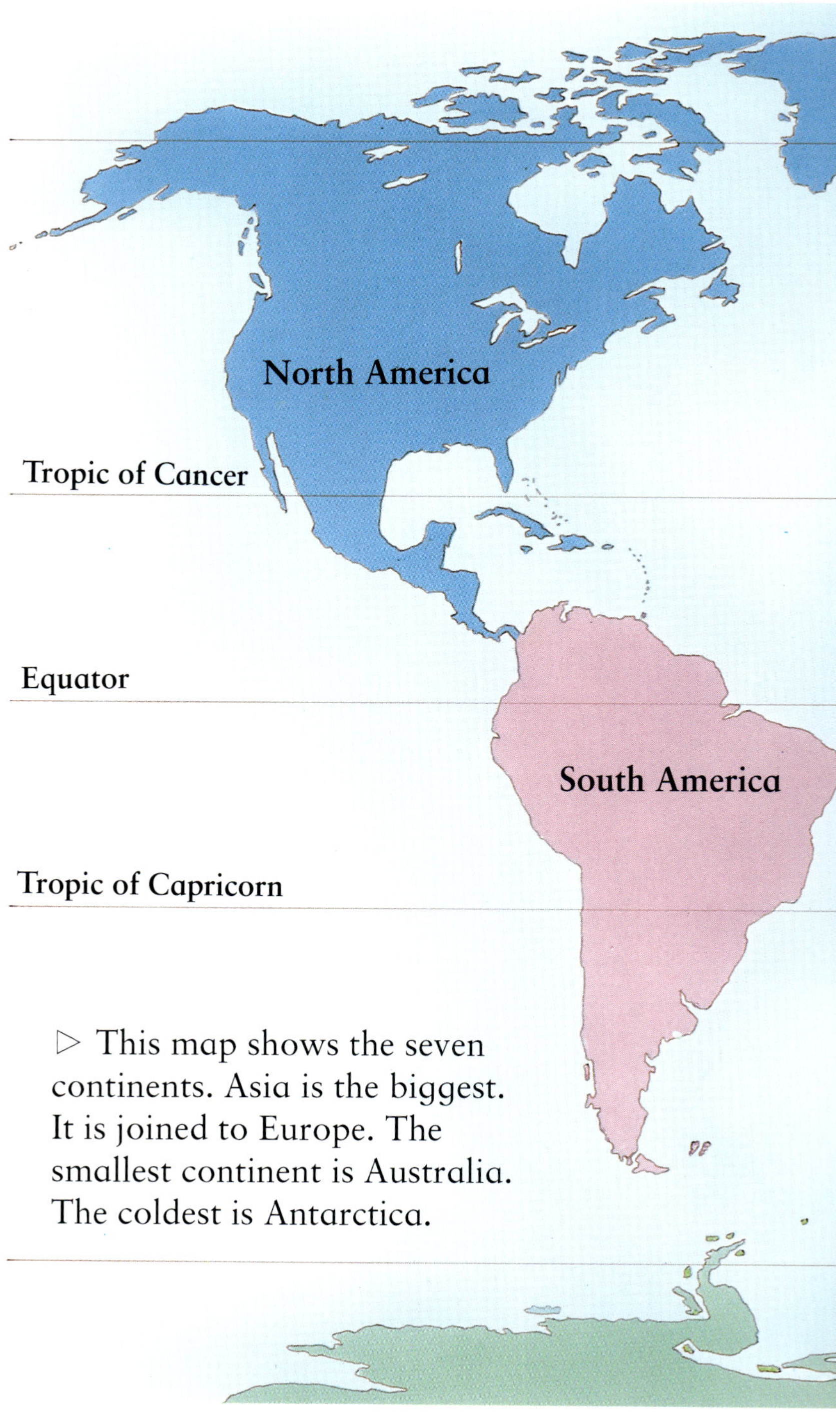

▷ This map shows the seven continents. Asia is the biggest. It is joined to Europe. The smallest continent is Australia. The coldest is Antarctica.

▽ On globes and maps a made-up line, called the Equator, divides the world in half. Countries nearest the Equator are the hottest.

▷ The world is round. To draw a flat map of it, mapmakers sometimes split its surface into several pieces as if peeling an orange.

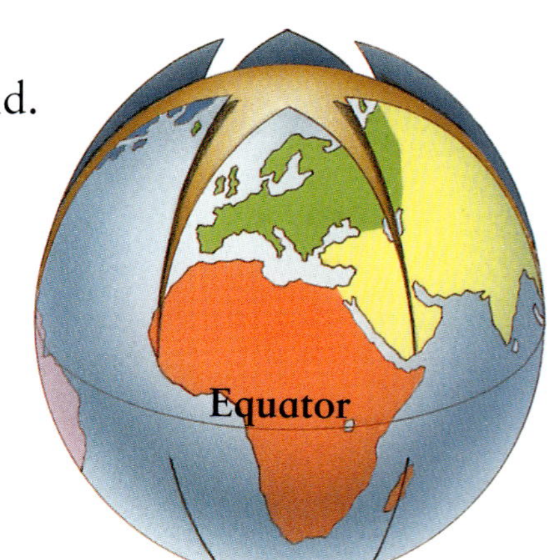

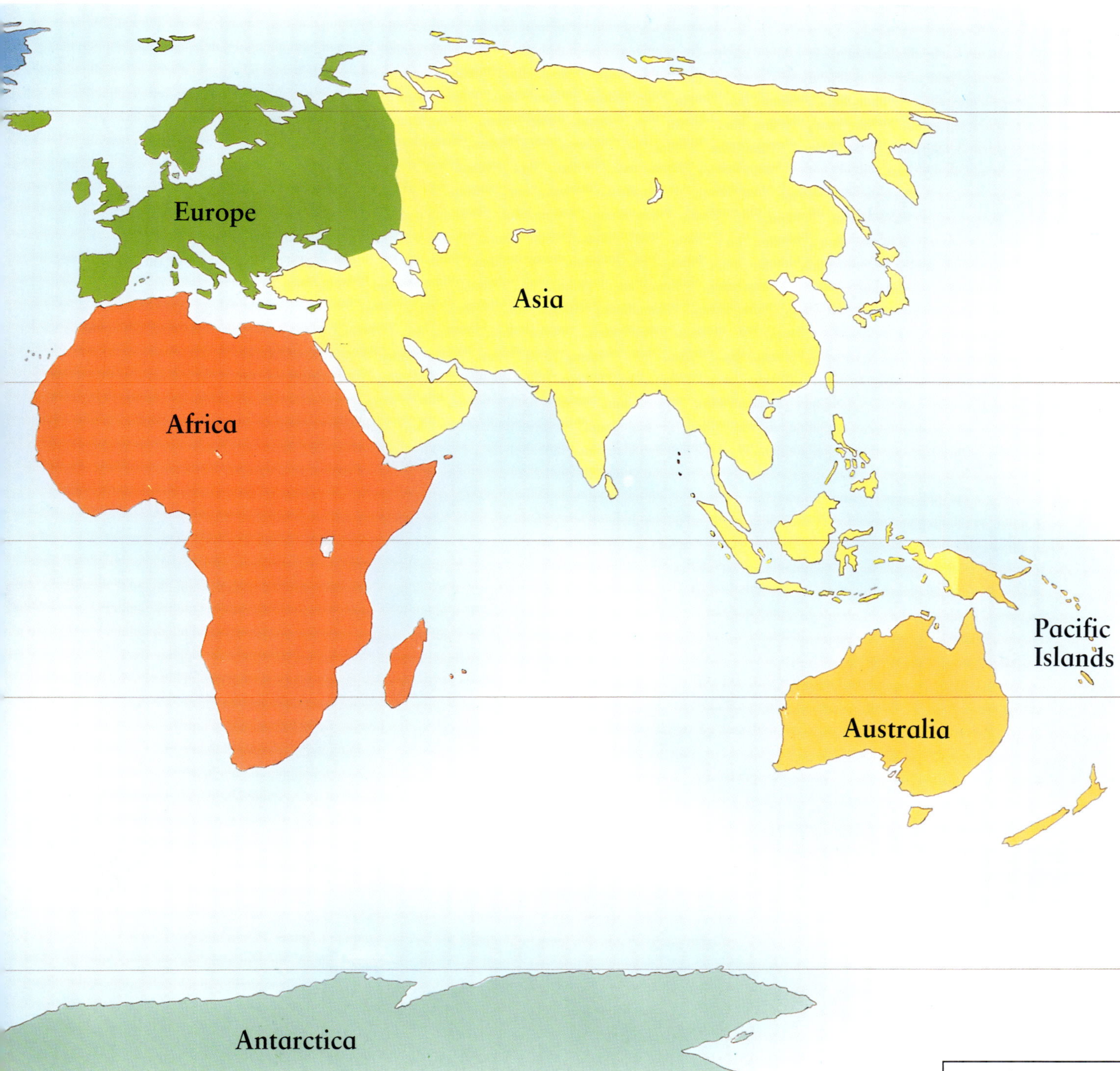

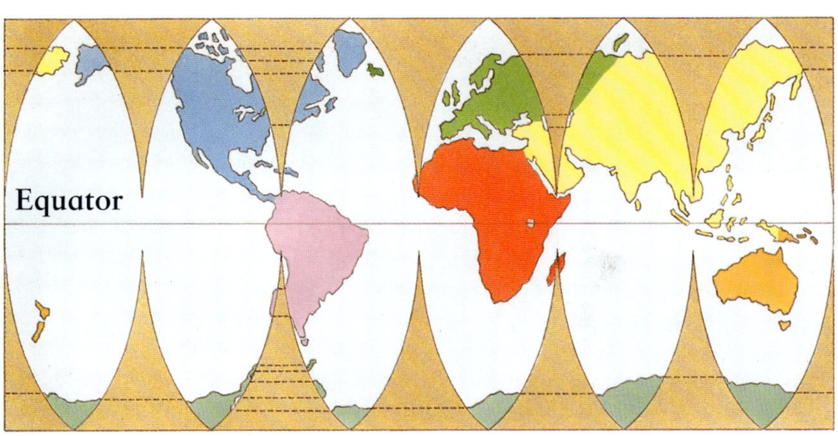

◁ The pieces are laid flat like this. But this shows that no flat map can show the curved surface of the world properly.

Find out more

Africa
Antarctica and Arctic
Asia
Australia and the Pacific Islands
Europe
Maps
North America
South America

Writing

Writing is very useful. It is a way of marking down words and ideas so that people can read them. Writing may be made up of little pictures or signs. It may be made up of letters of the alphabet. Each letter stands for one sound. Joining the letters together makes words.

△ This writing is on baked tablets of clay. It tells us what was in the storeroom of a Greek palace, such as weapons and chariot wheels.

नमस्ते
Hindi

Здравствуйте
Russian

مرحباً
Arabic

שלום
Hebrew

你好
Mandarin

△ This is how "Hello" is written in several different languages. Each one uses its own special alphabet.

△ You use words to write letters, messages, lists and stories. Writing helps you to remember and share your thoughts and ideas.

▷ Blind people can read by touching pages of raised dots. Each letter is a different pattern of dots. This is known as Braille.

Find out more

Books
Stories

X-ray

X-rays are invisible beams that can look through things that we cannot see through. Dentists and doctors use X-rays to take pictures of our teeth and inside our bodies. Bones show up very clearly on an X-ray. X-ray machines at airports can see inside bags to check what is inside.

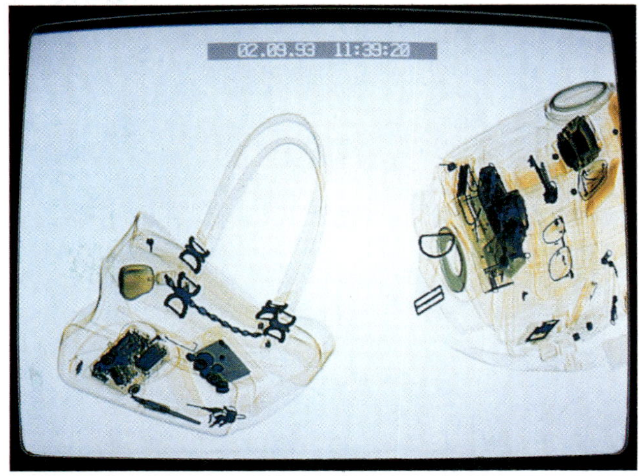

△ At the airport, luggage is put through an X-ray machine to check for metal weapons. Any guns or knives show up on the screen.

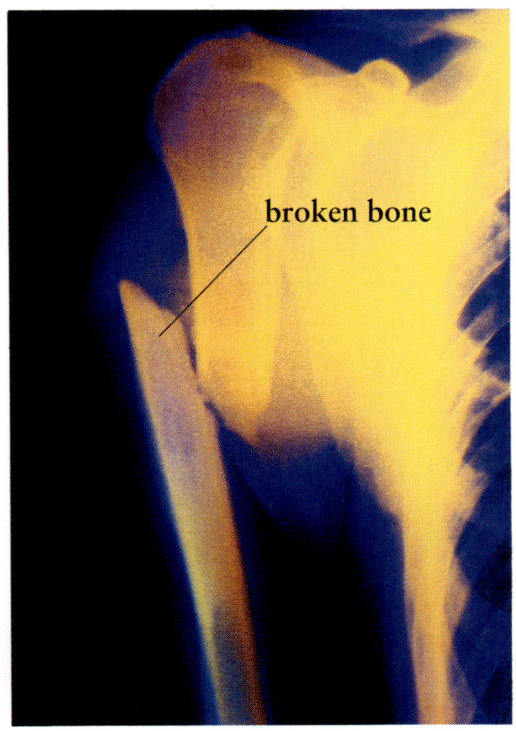

◁ Doctors use X-rays to find out if a bone is broken. They are careful to only use X-rays when necessary, as too many are not good for you.

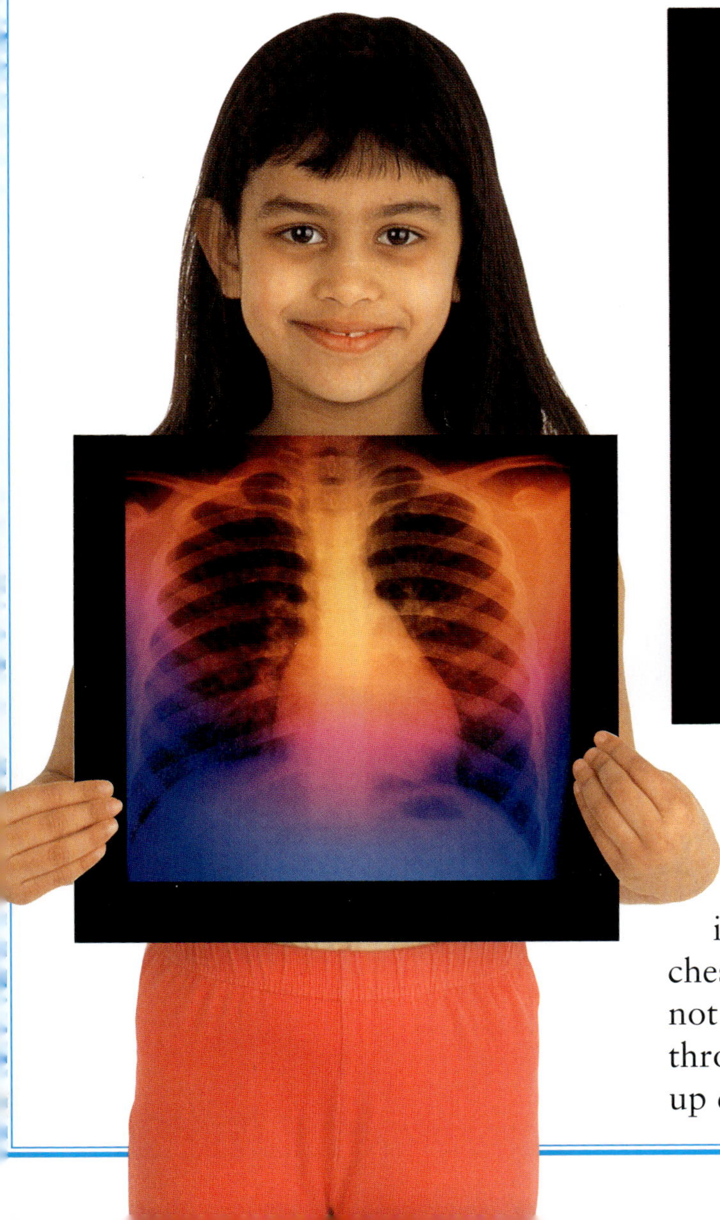

◁ This X-ray picture shows the inside of this girl's chest. The bones do not let the X-rays pass through, so they show up as white shadows.

Find out more

Human body
Light

Year

A year is a length of time. A year has 365 days. The days are divided into 12 months. Every four years, an extra day is added. This is called a leap year. Throughout the year, celebrations take place all over the world. These may remember important things that have happened during a country's history or celebrate the changing of the seasons.

△ July 4th is Independence Day in the United States. Americans celebrate this day with parades, marching bands, picnics, pageants and fireworks.

▷ Chinese New Year is celebrated between January and February. People dress up and set off noisy firecrackers in the street.

▽ Each year, you probably have a birthday party to celebrate the day you were born. Which day is yours on?

Find out more

Babies
Moon
Seasons

Zoo

Zoos are places where wild animals are kept for people to look at and learn about. Many zoos keep animals in big, open areas where they can roam about. They look after and breed animals that are in danger of dying out. But bad zoos keep animals in small, dirty cages.

△ Once there were no Père David's deer alive in the wild. Luckily, they were bred successfully in zoos and now live on the grasslands of China.

▽ Pandas are getting rarer and rarer in the wild. A few live in zoos where everyone hopes they will breed.

◁ Tamarin monkeys live in the rainforests of Brazil. In a good zoo animals live in areas that look like their wild homes.

Find out more

Animals
Conservation

Glossary

A **glossary** is a list of useful words. Some of the words used in this book may be new to you and so they are explained again here.

aborigines the first people to live in a country. Usually this means Australian Aborigines.

ancestor a person who lived in your family before you.

arteries and **veins** arteries are tubes inside the human body that carry blood away from the heart and veins are tubes that carry blood towards it.

atmosphere the layer of air that surrounds Earth. It contains the oxygen we breathe and protects us from the Sun's dangerous rays.

billion one million million.

border the line where one country ends and another country begins.

capital city a country's most important city. It is usually the city from which the government rules.

chrysalis the stage in the life of a butterfly or moth between the adult and caterpillar stages.

conifer a tree, such as a pine or fir tree, that carries its seeds in cones.

continent one of the seven large areas of land. They are: Africa, Antarctica, Asia, Australia, Europe, North America, South America.

deciduous when a tree loses all its leaves once a year in autumn.

effort and **force** effort is the work done to move something. A force pushes or pulls an object in a particular direction.

evergreen a tree that has leaves on it all year round.

generator a machine used to make electricity.

hibernation when an animal sleeps through the winter.

migration when an animal moves from one place to another each year.

mineral any natural material found in the ground that does not come from a plant or an animal.

orbit the curved path of an object that travels around a star or a planet.

oxygen a type of gas found in air. We need to breathe in oxygen in order to live. Our bodies use oxygen and food to make energy.

pole the most northern and southern points on Earth. Each end of a magnet is also called a pole.

prehistoric a very long time ago, before human history was written down.

prey animals that are hunted and killed by another animal for food.

static electricity electricity that does not run along wires in a steady current. Lightning is static electricity. It happens when electricity builds up in clouds and then leaps to the ground. Rubbing a balloon on a jumper makes static electricity.

submersible a small submarine, used especially for underwater exploration.

vibration when something moves backwards and forwards very quickly.

water vapour water is usually a liquid, but it can also be a solid (called ice) or a gas, called water vapour.

Index

This index helps you to find the subjects in this book. It is in alphabetical order. Main entries are in **dark**, or **bold**, letters. This is where you will find the most information on your subject.

The publishers would like to thank the following for contributing to this book:

Photographs

Page **6** Spectrum Colour Library; **7** Spectrum Colour Library *t*, Planet Earth Pictures *m*; **15** NHPA *t*, Brian and Cherry Alexander *bl*, TRIP *m*; **16** Bridgeman Art Library *l*, Archiv für Kunst und Geschichte *b*; **17** © ARS, NY and DACS, London 1996 *b*, Bridgeman Art Library *tr*; **19** NHPL; **20** Lawson Woods; **21** Images *t*, Spectrum Colour Library *b*; **22** Robert Harding *l*, Lupe Cunha Pictures *r*; **36** Science Museum/Science and Society Picture Library; **37** Trip *t*, Science Photo Library *r*; **47** Natural History Museum; **51** Telegraph Colour Library *t*, Image Select *r*; **53** Zefa *t*, Spectrum Colour Library *b*; **60** Mary Evans Picture Library; **70** Zefa *l*, Colorific *r*; **71** Spectrum Colour Library *t*, Image Select *r*; **72** Spectrum Colour Library *m*, Image Select *b*; **73** AKG Photo *t*, Greg Evans International *m*; **83** Hutchison Library *l*, Colorific *r*; **94** Zefa *l*, Telegraph Colour Library *b*; **95** Alamy, Corbis, Liam Muir; **97** Zefa; **100** Dognall Worldwide; **101** Images *r*, Colorific *l*; **102** Zefa; **98** Greg Evans International; **110** Rex Features; **111** Colorific; **112** Colorific *t*, Circa Photo Library *l*; **113** Telegraph Colour Library *ml*, TRIP *tr*; **122** Liam Muir *mr*; **125** Zefa *bl*, Cine Contact *t*; **130** Greg Evans International *l*, Allsport USA *r*; **131** Allsport; **133** Ronald Grant *b*, © 1996 Marvel Characters Inc. *m*; **139** Science Photo Library; **147** Zefa *m*, Zefa *r*; **148** Zefa; **152** Gilda Pacitti *b*; **153** Telegraph Colour Library *t*, Science Photo Library *b*

All other commissioned photographs Tim Ridley

Artists

Hemesh Alles, Craig Austin, Julian Baker, Bob Bampton, Julie Banyard, John Barber, Peter Barrett, Richard Bonson, Maggie Brand, Eric T Budge, John Butler, Lynn Chadwick, Harry Clow, Stephen Conlin, David Cook, Bob Corley, Peter Dennis, Maggie Downer, Richard Draper, Michael Fisher, Eugene Fleury, Roy Flooks, Chris Forsey, Rosamund Fowler, Mark Franklin, Andrew French, Terry Gabbey, Michael Gaffrey, Lee Gibbons (Wildlife Art Agency), Tony Gibbons, Mike Gillah, Peter Goodfellow, Ruby Green, Craig Greenwood, Peter Gregory, Ray Grinaway, J Haysom, Tim Hayward (Bernard Thornton Artists), Steven Holmes, Adam Hook, Christa Hook, Biz Hull, Mark Iley, Ian Jackson, Ron Jobson (Kathy Jakeman), Kevin Jones, BL Kearley, Roger Kent (Garden Studio), Deborah Kindred, Mike Lacey, Stuart Lafford, Terence Lambert, R Lewington, Bernard Long (Temple Rogers), S McAllinson, Angus McBride, Doreen McGuinness (Garden Studio), B McIntyre, Kevin Maddison, Mainline Design, Alan Male (Linden Artists), Shirley Mallinson, Maltings Partnership, David Marshall (Simon Girling and Associates), Janos Marffy, Josephine Martin, Tony Morris, Maggie Mundy Illustrators Agency, Steve Noon, Oxford Illustrators, Nicki Palin, Alex Pang, Darren Pattenden, Bruce Pearson, Clive Pritchard, Sebastian Quigley (Linden Artists), Elizabeth Rice, J Rignall, Bernard Robinson, Eric Robson, Eric Rowe, Liz Sawyer, Brian Smith, Guy Smith (Mainline), Annabel Spencely, Clive Spong, Paul Stangroom, Roger Stewart, Treve Tamblin, Myke Taylor (Garden Studios), Simon Tegg, Ian Thompson, Ross Watton, Graham White, Ann Winterbotham, David Wright

Models

Afua Arhin, Akua Arhin, Kirsty Bailey, Jack Clements, Sheila Clewley, Ceci Cole, Christopher Davies, James Fenwick, Hugo Flaux, Laurie Flaux, Toby Flaux, Ella Fraser, Olivia Gardner, Jessie Grisewood, John Grisewood, Katie Hill, Lucy Hill, Flora Kent, Josh Kent, Alexander Kendall, Fay Killick, Mia Mackinnon, Emma Makinson, Lucy Makinson, Hannah Mitchell, Georgina Ratnatunga, Louis Robertson, James Sullivan, Claire Tolman, Nicholas Tolman, Tom Whittington

Scallywags:
Gemma Loke, Meera Patel, Dwayne Thomas, Ahmani Vidal-Simon, David Watts, Jordan White

Tiny Tots to Teens:
Lauren Charles, Ken King, Jose Oliveira

Truly Scrumptious Ltd:
Nicholas Loblack, Tara Saddiq, Milo Taylor